DRAMATIC PAUSES

YOUTH SPECIALTIES TITLES

Professional Resources
The Church and the American Teenager (previously released as Growing Up in America)
Developing Spiritual Growth in Junior High Students
Help! I'm a Sunday School Teacher!
Feeding Your Forgotten Soul
Help! I'm a Volunteer Youth Worker!
High School Ministry
How to Recruit and Train Volunteer Youth Workers (previously released as Unsung Heroes)
Junior High Ministry (Revised Edition)
The Ministry of Nurture
Organizing Your Youth Ministry
Peer Counseling in Youth Groups
Advanced Peer Counseling in Youth Groups
The Youth Minister's Survival Guide
Youth Ministry Nuts and Bolts
Equipped to Serve
One Kid at a Time

Discussion Starter Resources
Amazing Tension Getters
Get 'Em Talking
High School TalkSheets
Junior High TalkSheets
High School Talk Sheets: Psalms and Proverbs
Junior High TalkSheets: Psalms and Proverbs
More High School TalkSheets
More Junior High TalkSheets
Option Plays
Parent Ministry TalkSheets
Tension Getters
Tension Getters Two
Would You Rather…?

Ideas Library
Ideas Combo 1-4, 5-8, 9-12, 13-16, 17-20, 21-24, 25-28, 29-32, 33-36, 37-40, 41-44, 45-48, 49-52, 53, 54
Ideas Index

Youth Ministry Programming
Adventure Games
Compassionate Kids
Creative Bible Lessons
Creative Programming Ideas for Junior High Ministry
Creative Socials and Special Events
Dramatic Pauses
Facing Your Future
Good Clean Fun
Good Clean Fun, Volume 2
Great Fundraising Ideas for Youth Groups
Great Games for City Kids
Great Ideas for Small Youth Groups
Great Retreats for Youth Groups
Greatest Skits on Earth
Greatest Skits on Earth, Volume 2

Holiday Ideas for Youth Groups (Revised Edition)
Hot Illustrations for Youth Talks
Hot Talks
Junior High Game Nights
More Junior High Game Nights
On-Site: 40 On-Location Youth Programs
Play It! Great Games for Groups
Play It Again! More Great Games for Groups
Road Trip
Super Sketches for Youth Ministry
Teaching the Bible Creatively
Teaching the Truth About Sex
Up Close and Personal: How to Build Community in Your Youth Group

4th-6th Grade Ministry
Attention Grabbers for 4th-6th Graders
4th-6th Grade TalkSheets
Great Games for 4th-6th Graders
How to Survive Middle School
Incredible Stories
More Attention Grabbers for 4th-6th Graders
More Great Games for 4th-6th Graders
Quick and Easy Activities for 4th-6th Graders
More Quick and Easy Activities for 4th-6th Graders
Teach 'Toons

Clip Art
ArtSource Volume 1—Fantastic Activities
ArtSource Volume 2—Borders, Symbols, Holidays, and Attention Getters
ArtSource Volume 3—Sports
ArtSource Volume 4—Phrases and Verses
ArtSource Volume 5—Amazing Oddities and Appalling Images
ArtSource Volume 6—Spiritual Topics
Youth Specialties Clip Art Book
Youth Specialties Clip Art Book, Volume 2

Video
Edge TV
God Views
The Heart of Youth Ministry: A Morning with Mike Yaconelli
Next Time I Fall in Love Video Curriculum
Promo Spots for Junior High Game Nights
Resource Seminar Video Series
Understanding Your Teenage Video Curriculum
Witnesses

Student Books
Going the Distance
Grow for It Journal
Grow for it Journal Through the Scriptures
How to Live with Your Parents Without Losing Your Mind
I Don't Remember Dropping the Skunk, But I Do Remember Trying to Breathe
Next Time I Fall in Love
Next Time I Fall in Love Journal
101 Things to Do During a Dull Sermon

DRAMATIC PAUSES

20 ready-to-use sketches for youth ministry

JIM HANCOCK

 ZondervanPublishingHouse
Grand Rapids, Michigan

A Division of *HarperCollins* Publishers

Dramatic Pauses: 20 ready-to-use sketches for youth ministry

Copyright © 1995 by Youth Specialties, Inc.

Books are published by Youth Specialties, Inc., 1224 Greenfield Drive,
92021.

brary of Congress Cataloging-in-Publication Data

Hancock, Jim, 1952-
　　Dramatic Pauses: 20 ready-to-use sketches for youth ministry / Jim Hancock
　　　　p.　cm.
　　ISBN 0-310-20718-5
　　1. Drama in Christian Education. 2. Christian drama, American. 3. Church work
with youth. 4. Amateur plays. I. Title
BV1534.4.H26 1995
246′.7—dc20   95-18768
                                                                          CIP

Edited by Noel Becchetti and Lorraine Triggs
Typography and design by Patton Brothers Design

Printed in the United States of America

96 97 98 99/ ML /5 4 3 2

Contents

Stage Directions...7

Introduction 9

Crystal 13

Cheryl and Tom are having it out over Tom's drug use. Cheryl's about ready to blow the whistle on Tom—but it will cost her ...*Crystal* runs around three minutes.

Germaine 17

Germaine is sixteen, maybe seventeen years old and at the end of her rope. She's been around the block—using alcohol, nicotine, food and sex to medicate her pain. *Germaine* runs about six and a half minutes.

Getting Buzzed 25

A kid answers questions about the progression of his drug use and is *buzzed* by a game show buzzer every time he gives a wrong answer. *Getting Buzzed* runs about three minutes.

Grace Under Pressure...29

A high school girl struggles with what to do when her class assignment is too close to the truth of her own tragedy. *Grace Under Pressure* runs close to eight minutes.

The Innkeeper...37

An Innkeeper confronts the usual suspects on Christmas eve, but in a somewhat unusual manner. *The Innkeeper* runs about four minutes.

Jenny...43

A girls talks about the gossip she heard at school and the truth of the matter. *Jenny* runs about four minutes.

Kim's Christmas...47

A sibling describes a painful Christmas scene and leaves us wondering about what comes next. *Kim's Christmas* runs a couple of minutes.

Losing...51

A lone speaker recounts the pain of losing to someone he (or she) trusted. *Losing* runs about a minute and a half.

Meet the Fines...53

It's Nicole's birthday and her older brother—still hanging around the house—is making trouble for the whole family. *Meet the Fines* runs around six minutes.

Rinse the Blood Off My Toga: Episode One 61

Gluteus Maximus, a private detective in ancient Rome, tries to solve the murder of Julius Caesar. *Rinse the Blood Off My Toga* is here revised as five episodes, each running fivish minutes.

Rinse the Blood Off My Toga: Episode Two 67

Rinse the Blood Off My Toga: Episode Three..................................73

Rinse the Blood Off My Toga: Episode Four..................................81

Rinse the Blood Off My Toga: Episode Five..................................87

The Boy..................................93

Five people in a small town talk about a boy we'll never see. As they reminisce about The Boy, a painful story emerges. *The Boy* runs around thirteen minutes.

Twelve Ways to Say No! 107

Twelve light-hearted ways of saying *no* to risky behavior are demonstrated, culminating with a pie in the face. *Twelve Ways to Say No!* runs about a minute and a half.

Vows..................................111

Addiction asks kids to promise to follow through to the end on what they're beginning. Which is not quite what the kids had in mind. *Vows* runs about two minutes.

You Think You're Alone 115

A kid confides to the audience that he or she has never really done any high-risk behaviors. A series of others offer reassurance that our speaker is not alone. *You Think You're Alone* runs about two minutes.

EXTRA HELPINGS

Two lengthier playlets for the adventurous and enthusiastic.

Beautiful Dreamer..................................119

Seventeen-year-old Joseph is the apple of his father's eye and the pain in his brothers' collective neck. The brothers fake his death and sell him into slavery. Years later, through miraculous acts of God and a whole lot of weird stuff, Joseph turns out to be the guy who saves Egypt from the effects of a grave famine. Coincidentally, he ends up saving his estranged family as well. *Beautiful Dreamer* runs around forty minutes.

Christmas Dreams..................................161

Joe and Maria are middle-aged folk preparing for another Christmas. Trouble is, Joe is so distracted by what's going on at work that he hasn't really thought about Christmas. Maria, on the other hand, is caught up in the details to the point that she may very well organize the meaning right out of Christmas. *Christmas Dreams* runs about half an hour, depending on the songs you choose.

Stage Directions

UPSTAGE

STAGE
RIGHT

CENTER
STAGE

STAGE
LEFT

DOWNSTAGE

AUDIENCE

Remember: Stage directions are from the
point of view of an actor looking at the audience.

Introduction

Most of us like good storytelling better than good sermonizing.

We're on our guard during a sermon. The preacher wants us to do something we don't want to do, or stop doing something we rather enjoy.

The storyteller asks only that we suspend our disbelief for a few minutes. And a good story, well-told, makes that easy. Once we let down our guard, the storyteller can take us just about anywhere and tell us nearly anything.

So I relish good stories, monologues, dialogues, vignettes, sketches, plays. I enjoy a good sermon—don't get me wrong. But I *love* a good story.

For a long time, I resisted an urge to write stories. I wasn't sure I knew enough about life to write believable plots. I was certain I didn't know enough to write authentic dialogue. Still, I kept inventing plots and characters in my head. And I listened to the way people talk—the rhythm and surge of speech, its fragments and pace.

Eventually, the urge to give voice and action to characters I invented overcame my fear of failing. I tried my hand writing sketches for kids to perform at youth groups and camps. They worked. Messages I had failed to communicate as a teacher or preacher slipped past the defenses of audience after audience. People were moved to feel and think in ways they hadn't planned on.

So I wrote more. I wrote sketches, monologues and plays for our youth group, for camps and retreats, for a high school drama group we called *Shadowlands Theatre*. I wrote for junior and senior high school assemblies and, then, for the screen. On our best days, the effects are startling.

Part of that effect is on those who see the scripts performed. I've yet to write any great theater; but a little storytelling goes a long way and that's what drama is—a story.

There is another effect I'm interested in because I'm a youth worker. Dramatic storytelling changes the performers and crew. Everyone likes to be part of something that makes a difference. And the point of the play is seldom lost on the people who bring it to life.

I, of course, was most profoundly affected. The stories in this book, and more like them, force me to pay attention and learn and change. Or else stop writing.

I suppose they also drove me to a change of profession. For about eight years I was a youth worker who wrote. Today I am a writer who does youth ministry. My day job is writing films and videos—especially *EdgeTV*. I spend free time working with kids in and around the church.

The stories collected here, and perhaps more later, are offered in the hope that they'll help you reach kids as they've helped me.

WHAT YOU'LL FIND HERE

Some of these pieces are barely two minutes long. One runs over forty minutes. Some of the dialogues can easily be read as a monologues—especially if you've got a Speech and Debate kid in your group. In most cases gender is irrelevant—or you can render it irrelevant by a re-write.

Most of this material can be performed nicely as Readers Theater (everybody on script). Of course, you have permission to copy scripts for your cast and crew—though I'll really appreciate it if you don't make copies for your friends.

For the most part these scripts are open-ended. These stories are meant to start people thinking, not stop them. They are designed as illustrations for talks, as discussion-starters, as denial-busters. The best of them are time-release truth capsules that keep working for hours. I haven't drawn many conclusions because drawing conclusions to stories is not the business of the storyteller but of the one who, having suspended disbelief, must come back to the real world and decide what to *do*.

Finally, I suppose I've left these scripts open-ended because, though I know kids, I don't know *your* kids. If you feel compelled to draw conclusions, draw them yourself in discussion or in your own wrapup.

You won't find much stage direction. I assume you'll flesh things out according to your situation. We've performed most of this material without sets and under every kind of lighting from full stage lights to putting someone at the wall switch to turn the overheads off and on.

If you've done some drama, you'll notice I chose an alternative format. These scripts are formatted like screenplays. I did that for two reasons: First, screenplay margins are easier to scan so actors learn lines faster. Second, as a rule of thumb, a page of screenplay dialogue takes about one minute to read. Therefore, you can *guesstimate* the length of a script by the number of pages. However, your mileage may vary. My characters tend to interrupt each other and some scripts read faster than a minute a page.

There's nothing sacred in this collection. If you can improve on anything, by all means, do it! Add, subtract, alter, modify with my blessing. Just, please, don't steal me blind.

GETTING YOUR ACTORS TOGETHER

If there's any magic to getting a troupe together, I don't know it. Of course, it helps having experienced people in the mix, but the only way to get experience is by **doing** it. So, if you haven't already got your group together…

I don't recommend beginning with a Big Production. That will take weeks at a minimum—more likely months—to produce. Big Productions can become all-consuming. If you don't watch out, you find that (in a different way than MacBeth had in mind) *the play's the thing*. It's probably not worth it.

Start simply. Find out who reads well and help them polish a monologue or simple dialogue in Readers Theater. Build from there. Spice your talks with drama; replace them with drama; see if anyone misses your one-person show.

As the enterprise grows, add to it. Get some lights. They don't have to be complicated. I've rigged simple, inexpensive systems and I'm an idiot about things mechanical and electrical. I've depended on stuff I bought at home improvement stores: outdoor halogen lamps patched by extension cords into a simple dimmer box a guy at church helped me build. Plug those babies in and let the show begin.

To my amazement, every time I've gotten a drama team together, we've had as many invitations to perform as we've cared to pursue. Pieces we developed for adolescent audiences got us invited to perform for single adults, Sunday night church, for groups across town, even public schools.

We never forced it; always took our time; let God do what God does.

We also never told anyone they couldn't be a part of the troupe. Some had no desire to be in front of the audience and were delighted to work with lights and music. Others struggled to pull their dramatic weight but—and this is the beauty of writing and adapting material for a group—we always found something meaningful for them to do.

In some ways, the best part has always been building a group of actors and crew who depended on each other and on Christ and who wanted to help people. What's not to like about that?

—Jim Hancock

Crystal

Crystal was written for a senior high school assembly. It came from encounters with people whose wheels were coming off after using crystal methamphetamine for a couple of years. Crystal is one of those synthetic drugs that people make up in the bathroom. It's very cheap and works really fast. Scary stuff. Among the effects—once the thrill is gone—are dramatic weight loss (an attraction for some), paranoia, hallucinations, delusions and heart palpitations. The latter symptoms seem to take more than a year to develop.

The last I heard, no one knew for sure whether or not the effects of Crystal are reversible.

SYNOPSIS

Cheryl and Tom are having it out over Tom's drug use. Cheryl's about ready to blow the whistle on Tom—but it will cost her …*Crystal* runs around three minutes.

NOTES

✻ Cheryl and Tom are in separate lights.

✻ They address the audience as if they were speaking to each other.

✻ Cheryl's light comes up first, then Tom's.

Crystal

CHERYL'S LIGHT UP

CHERYL
Tom, you're not *listening* to me!

TOM'S LIGHT UP

TOM
I *am* listening. You're *wrong*. You don't understand.

CHERYL
I am *not* wrong. You're *losing* it. I don't even *know* you anymore. You're never home; and when you *are*, you're locked in your room.

You lie to Mom and Dad—*and* me, Tom. You know how that makes me feel? You're nervous and cranky, and …*weird*. You're really getting weird.

TOM
Oh, that's just *great* —

CHERYL
[cutting in]
You don't think it's weird to nail your windows shut?

TOM
Cheryl …just shut up.

CHERYL
No! I mean it, Tommy. I'm scared.

TOM
Well *I'm* scared too. There's some very

spooky stuff goin' on.

I keep seeing this guy—it's like he's everywhere I go. I think he's following me. He *is* following me.

CHERYL
Oh, God, this isn't happening. You've got to get out of this. It's *crazy*!

You don't have time for your *friends* …*Vinnie* asked about you, Tom; he asks about you all the time. Why don't you return his calls?

TOM
Yeh, well, *Vinnie*. Vinnie *ditched* me. He has no idea what's happening here.

I saw him talking to that guy yesterday. I'm *sure* I saw him. I saw his picture—him and that guy. They were on this magazine at 7-11. It was so scary, Cher. I don't even know how they could know each other and they're on this *magazine*—together.

CHERYL
Stop it! Just *stop*! You're scaring me Tommy. I can't take this anymore.

I gotta tell somebody. I can't take this.

TOM
What the—*You* can't take it? *You*? You think this is *easy*?

My heart pounds *all* the time, Cher! My *lungs* are coming outta my chest! No way! You can't—

CHERYL
[cutting in]
Yes I can! I'm your sister and I love you and I *can* do it. I *will*.

TOM
Aw, *Cher* ...Not you too. *You* oughta understand. We smoked dope together. You got me drunk the first time ...If you *tell*, Mom and Dad will know everything, Cher. *Everything*.

CHERYL
[cutting in]
LISTEN TO ME!

I was wrong. You're over your head—

TOM
[cutting in]
Naw, that's not it. It's just ...I know what's goin' *on*, you know? I *know* what's goin' on...

CHERYL
No, Tom. No you don't. I'm really sorry.

CHERYL GOES TO BLACK

TOM
Cher? Let's work this out ...*Kay*?
We can work this out. I just have to get rid of that guy, you know? And make my heart slow down. Should I call the police about that guy? Whatdaya—oh *right*—they're prob'ly *in* on it. I'm scared, Cher...

Cher?

TOM GOES TO BLACK

Germaine

Germaine was written for a senior high retreat on *power*. It's a useful introduction (or interlude) on the subject of control. Germaine exercises personal power until it turns around and grabs her. It hasn't been hard to get people talking after they've met Germaine. By the way, Germaine eventually made her way onto the screen in *EdgeTV*.

SYNOPSIS

Germaine is, sixteen, maybe seventeen years old. She's been around the block—using alcohol, nicotine, food, sex, and various drugs to medicate her pain. Now, desperate, she comes clean.

Germaine runs about six and a half minutes.

NOTES

❋ If Germaine is the student body, it's more because she's been available than because she's beautiful or shapely. She might even show the struggle with weight that her habits would tend to create. Then again, she might have been on the crystal methamphetamine diet in which case she would probably have circles under her eyes.

❋ Germaine sits on a chair, shoulders hunched, palms down on the sides ofher seat, uncomfortable. Germaine speaks sometimes to the air, sometimes to herself.

❋ Germaine is at the end of her rope. The act of telling her story is desperate—something she never expected to do. She is tired and emotionally flat.

❋ The Voice comes from offstage. It is gentle, inviting.

Germaine

GERMAINE SITS ON A CHAIR, SHOULDERS HUNCHED, PALMS DOWN ON THE SIDES OF HER SEAT, UNCOMFORTABLE. GERMAINE SPEAKS SOMETIMES TO THE AIR, SOMETIMES TO HERSELF.

GERMAINE
I don't know what to say. I mean I don't know where to start.

THE VOICE COMES FROM OFFSTAGE. IT IS GENTLE, INVITING.

VOICE
Start at what you think is the beginning. Would that be ok?

GERMAINE
No. Yes; I guess.

I guess I think it started when I was twelve—thirteen maybe. It doesn't matter; it's just that one day I realized guys paid attention to me—older guys.

So one night I go to the movies and there's this long line and these guys drive by to see what's playing. And we start talking and stuff and pretty soon I get out of line and into the car. I left my friends there—I still can't believe that.

Anyway: we drive around and stuff ...and—and they got me a little drunk, and...

VOICE
It's ok...

GERMAINE

…and by the time I got back to the theater my friends were gone.

I walked home and made up some lie to my Mom…and she bought it.

VOICE

Why did you lie?

GERMAINE

I don't know. It was so awful but I felt guilty. I shouldn't have…I wish I hadn't done any of it. I wish…Oh man…

Anyway. Once I lied, I didn't know how to go back. So I didn't.
I was…well, she bought it so easily…I knew I could get away with stuff. So I did. I started meeting guys wherever.

VOICE

And…

GERMAINE

And…everything; anything. I don't know. It was like it wasn't even me. I'd let them do stuff and, I don't know, I guess I felt *loved* or *needed* or something.

It was weird. It *is* weird.

VOICE

That's something you didn't have? You didn't feel loved?

GERMAINE

Yeah, and I thought nobody needed me. I thought it didn't make any difference whether I lived in my house or not; or whether I went to school or not. It was like not being there.

VOICE
No difference to…?

GERMAINE
To anybody. To me. Just a second.

VOICE
And the boys…?

GERMAINE
And the boys…I had something the boys wanted. I learned to play the game so that, after a while, it was like I had something they *needed*. Do you know what I mean?

VOICE
I'm not sure.

GERMAINE
Yeah, well, I'm not sure either…

VOICE
Does it seem odd to you that you started doing something that was so painful to you? I mean, your introduction to sex was not exactly—I don't know—*fairy tale*.

GERMAINE
You got that right.

Did you ever hear that song *Sex As a Weapon*? It's like from the early eighties?

VOICE
I don't think so.

GERMAINE

I found it in my mother's tapes. It's about someone who controls people with sex—with love.

VOICE

Is that what you were doing?

GERMAINE

Yeah—well, kind've. It was more like *Sex As Money*. You know what I mean? I used sex to buy what I wanted—attention, I guess; and to feel needed…

VOICE

And did that work for you?

GERMAINE

In a way, for a while…I think I thought that if guys needed me I could have—I don't know—power over them, I guess. But it doesn't feel *right* now—here. It never really felt right. It felt *good*, at least some of the time, but it never really felt right.

VOICE

And there's a difference between feeling good and feeling good about yourself…

GERMAINE

Yeah. There's a difference.

VOICE

Which is…

GERMAINE

Which is that, when love—when even sex—is power, it's like it not love anymore. And that doesn't feel right. That doesn't make me feel good about myself—at all.

Am I making sense?

VOICE
You're making a lot of sense.

Ah...Where is God in all this?

GERMAINE
About a million miles away. I haven't talked to God about anything real for a long time. I've thought about it; but I haven't done it.

VOICE
How come?

GERMAINE
You have to ask?

. . . I did talk with God about one thing. I told him I wanted to die.

VOICE
And...

GERMAINE
He wouldn't let me.

VOICE
Why...did you decide to tell me this? What do you want to *do* about it?

GERMAINE
Why am I telling you this...I don't know exactly.

I know I've carried this alone for too long. I know I'm sick of it.

I know I tried to eat and drink and smoke and screw my brains out.

And here I am.

Nothing could be worse than this. I don't care anymore. Having my mom and stepfather find out? Doesn't matter.

I tried everything…But you're right: it's time to do somethin'. Maybe even… I don't know—*somethin'*.

TO BLACK

Getting Buzzed

Getting Buzzed was written for a senior high summer camp. It's been useful as a *denial buster*. It's an easy context for talking about the rationalizations and self-deception that many (most?) of us are familiar with. *Getting Buzzed* has less to do with drugs than with coming clean about why we do what we do. This sketch also found its way to *EdgeTV*.

SYNOPSIS

A kid answers questions about the progression of his drug use and is *buzzed* by a game show buzzer every time he gives a wrong answer. *Getting Buzzed* runs about three minutes.

NOTES

✸ The Questions come from off camera.

✸ The Kid addresses the audience.

✸ He is straight-looking. Jeans and t-shirt. Nothing druggy.

✸ After each response from the kid a game show buzzer goes off. You can also use an air horn, available at boat shops.

✸ Cut to black at the buzzer, then fade back up.

✸ At the end of the last beat, a red light flashes like a police light. You may have to experiment a little to come up with a suitable light. You could also tape a police siren to play at the end.

Getting Buzzed

THE QUESTION COMES FROM OFF CAMERA.

QUESTION
Why did you smoke your first cigarette?

THE KID ADDRESSES THE AUDIENCE.

KID
Well... I told Carlisle if he'd steal 'em, I'd smoke one. So then he stole some from his old lady and—I didn't wanna wimp out—so I kind've *had* to...

BUZZER AND CUT TO BLACK

LIGHTS UP

QUESTION
Why did you drink your first beer?

KID
Uh, lemme see. I was at this football party at my uncle's house and he says, "Here boy, this'll make a man outa ya!" and hands me one. I didn't want him to think I was a baby...so I drank it.

BUZZER AND CUT TO BLACK

LIGHTS UP

KID
Well just a minute, I **really** just sipped it. I didn't like the taste so I poured most of it in the john. And then I **pretended** that I liked it.

BUZZER AND CUT TO BLACK

LIGHTS UP

> QUESTION
> Why did you get drunk the first time?

> KID
> I remember that! And I wasn't really drunk! I just pre*tended* to be drunk, you see, 'cause I wanted everybody to *think* I was drunk...

BUZZER AND CUT TO BLACK

LIGHTS UP

> QUESTION
> Then why did you *really* first get drunk?

> KID
> Well, I was out with these guys fishing and stuff and beer was all they brought and I was thirsty and I didn't wanna leave to go find something to drink and I thought hey, weekends were made for Michelob or whatever and—

BUZZER AND CUT TO BLACK

LIGHTS UP

> QUESTION
> Why did you smoke your first joint?

> KID
> I, ah...I was drunk.

BUZZER AND CUT TO BLACK

LIGHTS UP

QUESTION
Why did you snort cocaine the first time?

KID
Get off me! I was curious, ok?

BUZZER AND CUT TO BLACK

AS WE FADE UP THE KID'S BACK IS TO THE AUDIENCE. THE VOICE GETS HIS ATTENTION WITH A COUGH AND WHEN HE TURNS AROUND HE IS SHUFFLING THROUGH A WAD OF MONEY.

KID
Oh, hey; I didn't hear you come in.

QUESTION
Why did you deal the first time?

KID
We-ell, it wasn't *dealing*. I just figured there was no reason I couldn't pay for my partying; you know what I'm saying?

BUZZER AND CUT TO BLACK

LIGHTS UP

QUESTION
And why did you get busted the first time?

KID
No man! See I've never *been* busted.

THE KID'S FACE REGISTERS SHOCK AS A FLASHING RED LIGHT TURNS ON, THE BUZZER SOUNDS, AND WE FADE TO BLACK.

Grace Under Pressure

Grace Under Pressure is a real story, told me by a young friend. I've used it as a reading to stimulate thinking about the cost of making a difference—or of *not* trying to make a difference. This script form takes the monologue a simple step further. Count on Grace's story to bring up some important stuff, including stories of sexual assault.

SYNOPSIS

A high school girl struggles with what to do when her class assignment is too close to the truth of her own tragedy. *Grace Under Pressure* runs close to eight minutes.

NOTES

* The Narrator is upstage left and addresses the audience.

* The Teacher is upstage right and addresses Grace.

* Grace is downstage center and addresses the audience.

* Separate lights for each character would be nice.

Grace Under Pressure

GRACE'S LIGHTS UP

GRACE

I never expected to find ignorance and prejudice in the classroom. It doesn't make sense. School is where people learn to think with open minds. Well, isn't it?

We were reading *Tess of the d'Urbervilles*. Thomas Hardy's insight into the aftermath of sexual violence surprised me. Writing when he did—the novel was published in 1891—Hardy wouldn't have found much about such matters in popular literature. But *Tess* is remarkably in touch with the shame and self-blaming that come from sexualized violence.

Tess was a victim of sexual assault; I have no doubt about that. Hardy didn't have to use the word "rape" to get the truth across. He put it over, under and between the lines.

But…not everyone saw what Hardy saw.

NARRATOR LIGHT UP

NARRATOR

If Grace was surprised that Thomas Hardy saw it clearly, she was more surprised that her classmates missed even the shadow of the truth about Tess. They took her shame for guilt and her self-doubt and second-guessing for responsibility. They laughed at Tess—said she was asking for it.

NARRATOR LIGHTS DOWN, GRACE LIGHTS UP.

GRACE

I'm *stunned*. This is not 1891; rape is no secret now. I'm *beyond* stunned. Does no one in this class understand what it feels like to be brutalized?

I mean, a punch in the nose is a shock; finding your car window broken and your stereo gone makes you feel violated. But sexual assault is in a class by itself. There is no more intimate crime and there's *nothing* funny about it.

GRACE LIGHTS DOWN, NARRATOR LIGHTS UP.

NARRATOR

Grace's pain turned to anger. She didn't want to go to class. She was sick of discussions with insensitive, ignorant, prejudiced people.

GRACE'S LIGHT COMES UP

GRACE

They have no idea…

NARRATOR

But Grace knew. She knew in the worst way what Thomas Hardy was saying.

GRACE

It was the summer after ninth grade. One of those "unknown assailant" things—not acquaintance rape. That's much more common but this was the stranger-in-the-dark thing. It doesn't happen very often, but…well, it happens.

NARRATOR
Grace's emotions came to a boil with a writing assignment.

TEACHER'S LIGHT COMES UP

TEACHER
Part One: put yourself in Tess's place. What does that feel like? What is her dilemma?

Part Two: write from the point of view of her attacker. What does *that* feel like?

GRACE
The first part is tough but doable. I don't wanna *think* about this, much less write about it. But if I have to…

But the second part—well that's just out of the question. The one place I will *not* go is inside the attacker's mind.

GRACE ADDRESSES HER TEACHER AS SHE CONTINUES

I can't do this.

TEACHER
[thoughtfully]
Okay. Give me two pages about, oh, anything autobiographical.

GRACE TURNS AWAY FROM THE TEACHER AND LOOKS GRATEFULLY TO HEAVEN. SHE MOUTHS THE WORDS

GRACE
Thank you.

NARRATOR

Grace was off the hook.

But not for long. A question nagged at her. Would the class be so hard on Tess if they knew that, right in the room, was someone who knew what she went through from the *inside*? Grace wondered…and then she wrote.

NARRATOR AND TEACHER LIGHTS GO DOWN

GRACE

I still remember.

I remember that night, two years ago; the three alarm fire, when no one had time for a frightened little girl leaning against a rough tree, utterly alone in the cold night. The little girl who had cried in pain and rage and hate—sure she must have done *something* to make that man do what he did. But not quite sure what.

I remember going to my grandparents' house, next to the inn where the fire raged on; cleaning myself up; swearing that no one would ever know what happened. Because I blamed myself, I thought everyone else would too—and they would hate me if they knew.

I survived the rest of the summer and most of the following school year by becoming reclusive and withdrawn. No one was allowed to get close to me because I was too afraid they would guess my secret—not only that I had been raped, but that I hated myself for it.

I hated myself with a passion I did not

understand. Unable to share my feelings with others, I spilled them into the toilet, acting out my hatred through bulimia. I was crying for help, but afraid to ask for it.

I got help, without asking. It came through the simple yet so difficult act of trying to kill myself.

The help came mainly in the form of my youth director. With God's help, he asked the right questions. He pointed me in the right direction and held my hand until I was strong enough to go on my own.

Slowly, I learned that I'm a person worth knowing. I found that I can do stupid things and not be a stupid person. I learned that what other people think of me has no reflection on who I am. This process led to my becoming a Christian, which showed me how to love myself.

Which is not to say the memory doesn't hurt. I cry when I see fire engines racing to a fire. I cry when ignorant kids in my English class laugh at Tess and say it was her fault she was raped. And I don't just cry. Sometimes I get angry, too. Angry at people who don't know, and don't care, about how a situation affects others.

Anger? Yes. Hurt? Of course. Hate?…Well, no. It's been a long journey, but…it hasn't been wasted.

THE TEACHER LIGHT COMES UP AND THE TEACHER ADDRESSES GRACE.

TEACHER
Perfect! This is wonderful! No, I *mean* it. Other kids made a joke of the assignment and I was planning to talk with the class about it. Your essay makes that much more powerful. We'll read it on Wednesday.

THE TEACHER LIGHT GOES DOWN.
GRACE ADDRESSES THE AUDIENCE.

GRACE
Good. That's the day before Thanksgiving. That gives me the long weekend to recover if it doesn't go well.

NARRATOR LIGHT UP

NARRATOR
But there was a substitute on Wednesday. Grace waited through the holiday, nervous, hoping that, in the end, it would be worth the risk.

NARRATOR LIGHT DOWN

GRACE
I dreaded the next class. When I arrived I found my teacher waiting.

TEACHER LIGHT UP AND THE TEACHER SPEAKS TO GRACE

TEACHER
Grace, I've decided not to read your paper. A lot of these people are just too immature...I'm afraid it would just be a slap in the face.

TEACHER LIGHT DOWN

GRACE

My emotions spun out of control. Sure, I was spared the embarrassment of hearing my words read out loud—But you missed the point! I took that risk for a *reason*. I *want* them to know. I *want* them to squirm.

You think you're protecting me, but you're just rescuing the class from the truth!

I've come too far…Oh, God, I've come too far. What'm I gonna do now?

TO BLACK

The Innkeeper

The Innkeeper was written for a Christmas pageant. Little kids sang before and during these monologues. Children played the roles of Mary and Joseph, the Shepherds and Wise Men. A couple of big kids played the front and rear end of a donkey and added a bit of levity to the beginning of the show. [The donkey let the audience know it was OK to laugh which made things much easier on the Innkeeper.] At the end of the show, we did the traditional candle-lighting ceremony in which everyone in the sanctuary passed a flame from candle to candle as we sang 'Silent Night."

The reaction to *The Innkeeper* astonished me. The little people had a fun time watching the story unfold, but the big people saw themselves. Come to think of it, I saw myself. It seemed to make a difference in how we all saw Christmas.

SYNOPSIS

An Innkeeper confronts the usual suspects on Christmas eve, but in a somewhat unusual manner. *The Innkeeper* runs about four minutes.

NOTES

* The Innkeeper addresses the audience. He can react to the kids in the pageant costumes.
* The Innkeeper can be done with a minimal set. A door frame for the Innkeeper's entrances and exits. A simple manger for the Baby.
* The scenes are separated by the appropriate Christmas carols or even cool recorded music and video or slides or dance or whatever you can imagine…
* In any event, we only hear the Innkeeper's half of the conversations.

The Innkeeper

As the lights come up the Innkeeper
reacts to Joseph and Mary.

Innkeeper

I have no room—I *told* you.

Yes, yes I understand you have come a
great distance. But distance does not create space. If you travelled from Jerusalem;
if you journeyed all the way from Rome,
it makes no difference if I have no room.

You do not believe me? Come inside and
see for yourself…But it is impossible.
Why? you may ask. Because I have no
room!

Of *course* I know how late it is! You call
me away from my guests. The house is
full. Go up the road; perhaps they can
help you.

Yes, yes, I *understand* your wife is with
child. Believe me, I *know*. It might be your
fat donkey as well as your wife and you
know my answer: I have no room.

Well, for the donkey perhaps.
There is a stable there in back. And, if a
man wishes to look after his
donkey…and if a woman wishes to look
after her husband on a cold night…who
am I to object…?

FADE OUT AND MUSIC

What is all this racket! And what is that sm…Ooh, shepherds!

What is your business here? The house is closed, we are all asleep! What mischief— What? Where? Washing your socks by night?

Oh, your flocks. Pity. Well no matter. What has this to do with me?

You don't say… *Angels*. Of all things… And so long after the taverns have closed.

Yes, yes, we all await the Savior. I daresay the Promised One *may* be proclaimed by angels. I *doubt* the announcement will come to a band of drunken sheep boys.

Yes, yes, of course it is my stable. Yes there is a manger, of *course*, a *manger*.

Eh? No, no, don't go in there! There are, ah, *animals*. They work hard they need their rest…*Off* with you!

He pulls back as if threatened.

Oh very well. If a band of drunken shepherds with, ah, sticks and clubs wish to compare sheep on a cold night…who am I to object ?

FADE OUT AND MUSIC.

AS THE LIGHTS COME UP THE INNKEEPER
REACTS TO THE KINGS.

Oh, my *Lords*…I, ah, I ah…

Forgive me; we don't see royalty in these parts. Here, ah, let me call the others, let us prepare something for you.

I, ah, beg your pardon, but I have no room. But, for *you*, my Lords, for you, my children can sleep in the kitchen, my wife and I can—*stay up*. We can do something, I know it.

Yes, my Lord? A star? Well, I am a simple man, but *yes*, now that you say it…

You don't say? All that way to seek a child king. I don't suppose there were *angels*? No, I thought not. A *star*…

A *stable*? Yes, of course there is a stable—in the back. But, my Lords, it is filled with, ah, *animals*—of the four-legged kind…And a growing number of the two-legged kind as well.

Of course, my Lords; as you wish. If a *king* wishes is to see a poor innkeeper's stable, who is the innkeeper to object?

FADE OUT AND MUSIC

AS THE LIGHT COMES UP THE INNKEEPER IS ON HIS
KNEES REACTING TO JESUS.

Oh, my LORD and my God….

Who could have *known*? Who would have guessed? Not I. I would never think;

never *imagine*; never *hope*...I, ah...I am without words.

But if the LORD of glory comes to visit a wretched man, who is that —who am *I*— to object?

FADE OUT

Jenny

Jenny was written for junior and senior high school assemblies. This little show is about finding the story behind the story. It's useful for talking about gossip and about the importance of helping friends in crisis. At first the audience may think that the *speaker* is Jenny. When they realize she is Jenny's new friend they are set up reconsider the nature and obligations of friendship.

SYNOPSIS

A girls talks about the gossip she heard at school and the truth of the matter. *Jenny* runs about four minutes.

NOTES

✱ The speaker is center stage.

✱ She sadly confides in the audience.

Jenny

I heard some people talking before school...I didn't really know any of them—I knew some faces...

They were talking about a new girl—said they heard she just came from someplace or other. "Interdistrict transfer," one of them was saying, like he really knew. Said she got quite a welcome on Friday night.

They said they heard it started at the mall; said this new girl was supposed to meet somebody there and was just hanging out, waiting.

There was an argument about what happened next, but they agreed that they'd *all* heard that she left with some guy she didn't know. Some of them said he was in eleventh grade and she was really drunk, and somebody heard she didn't really want to go at first, and somebody else said, "Yeah, right."

Everybody laughed.

I didn't want to be too obvious, and I *didn't* want to join them, but I couldn't hear. So I moved closer. This one guy was saying, "Yeah, like some chick is really gonna go behind the mall with a dude she doesn't know." But everybody else was saying "No! Swear to God! My friend told me!"

And then they were talking almost in a whisper about how this girl just went for it. Said she never even went back to the mall. Said she made it with like all this guys friends; said a security guard found her wandering around the parking lot later…

And then the bell rang. But I just stood there. I *knew* who they were talking about …

And it *wasn't* like they said! Jenny was waiting for *me*. We were meeting there and then going to a movie. I was running late and when I got there I couldn't find her anywhere and I thought, "Oh fine; *keep* me waiting!" And I just hung out in the mall with friends and stuff and waited for her. After a while I got really mad. And *then* I got really scared. I mean she was supposed to spend the night with me and everything. I didn't know what to do …I called my Mom and told her we were gonna stay to see the movie again and she said OK and she'd see us at 11:45.

It was after 11:00 when Jenny found me. I was *so* mad, and then I saw she was crying really hard and I said, "Jenny, what's wrong?"

It *wasn't* like they said. Jenny *wasn't* drunk; and she really *didn't* want to go with that guy. They were just kidding around. He said he recognized her from school and then he grabbed her purse and she chased him out the back door of the mall.

And it wasn't like she made it with all this guy's friends—it was *like* she was raped by this guy, and while he had her down another guy says, "I believe I'll have me somma that."

Can you believe that? The more the merrier, right?

She felt so stupid. I mean, she was, in pain and crying and too embarrassed to tell anybody why.

I kept saying, "It's not your fault, Jenny!" But I know she thinks it is. And I know she hasn't told her parents.

We managed to fake it with my mom and I'm pretty sure she doesn't suspect anything.

I'm sure Jenny hasn't told anybody.

And now I don't know what to do. She's new and *I* don't even know her all that well. I keep thinking, "Man, if I'd been on time..." And then I think, "This is crazy. I've gotta tell somebody." This is so bizarre.

SHE LOOKS TO THE BACK OF THE ROOM, MUTTERS TO THE AUDIENCE, THEN CALLS OUT

Oh my gosh, there she is. Oh my gosh.

Jenny, we gotta talk!

TO BLACK

Kim's Christmas

Kim's Christmas was written as part of a talk on refusing the grace of God. It's sort of strange and leaves people a bit unsettled— ready, I think, for the question, *Why would anybody resent a gift just because it wasn't what they hoped for? Is it stubbornness? Is it self-centeredness?* Does Kim have a legitimate grievance? Is this really so far out?

SYNOPSIS

A sibling describes a painful Christmas scene and leaves us wondering about what comes next. *Kim's Christmas* runs a couple of minutes.

NOTES

❋ The speaker addresses the audience.

❋ The speaker can be male or female.

Kim's Christmas

A strange thing happened last Christmas.

My sister, Kimmy, wanted *something*. It's funny; I'm not sure I even know what it was. But she *wanted* it, whatever it was, and she didn't get it.

We all gathered around the tree, you know, like every other year. And my Dad played Santa and it was like Kim was so impatient to get to the package from Mom and Dad. She insisted on opening that one first—you know, she just piled the others around her, waiting for the Big One.

When Dad passed it across, she tore into the wrapping like a wild woman…And her face changed. There was surprise, maybe even shock. I thought: "She is *so* happy."

But that wasn't it. The surprise turned sour on her face—then angry. She gave us all that *look*.

I'm not sure anyone else noticed. They were all tearing open packages and Grandpa was looking amused, and everybody was excited.

Kim just sat there; cold.

Dad realized everyone else was about done and Kim hadn't touched another gift. He said, "Come on, Toots. You better put it in gear!"

She didn't look at him; just said "I don't feel well," and walked out.

Dad called after her: "Hey, Santa's gonna take your stuff back!" Like he could kid her out of it.

She said, "He can have it."

And that was it. Later in the day, Mom put Kim's presents in the closet; said she could open them when she was ready.

My little brother said, "It's probably her period."

But it wasn't. It was some deep down disappointment; a bitterness she couldn't—maybe wouldn't—shake. I don't know.

I haven't looked for a while; as far as I know, Kim's presents are still in the closet; still unopened.

I don't know…This has been a hard year for Kim—for all of us really.

TO BLACK

Losing

Losing was part of a talk on forgiving. It later found its way into a resource called *The Rock and Roll Teacher*. *Losing* is about the cost of forgiving.

SYNOPSIS

A lone speaker recounts the pain of losing to someone he (or she) trusted. *Losing* runs about a minute and a half.

NOTES

* The speaker confides in the audience.

* The speaker's gender is unimportant.

* The *he*'s can be changed to *she*'s.

Losing

It's not what he did, you know.

It's that *he* did it.

If it were someone else, I think I could shake it off.

But it's not. It's the person I trust— trusted…most in the world.

And I can't just let it go. It's like a video- tape that replays over and over. And every time it comes out the same…

I lose.

But it isn't just the losing. It's the way I've lost—it's losing to him: my *friend*.

I'd like to just forget it—*really*. I'd like to *wash* it out of my mind and move on.

But I can't because now he owes me— big time. I can't rest till it's right—until everybody knows *I'm* right…

And he's wrong.

I don't know how much longer I can do this. It wakes me up in the morning; I eat it for lunch; every night it talks to me in my sleep.

I'm sick to death of the whole thing. I want to be done with it. But it won't let go…

I can't *let* it go…

TO BLACK

Meet The Fines

Meet the Fines was written on a whim. It could be subtitled *Is it Just Me or Is there an Elephant in the Living Room?* The Fines are deeply in denial about something. We don't get to know what, exactly, but when push comes to shove they back down from conflict. Maybe your audience will have an idea or two.

SYNOPSIS

It's Nicole's birthday and her older brother—still hanging around the house—is making trouble for the whole family. *Meet the Fines* runs around six minutes.

NOTES

* Nicole is in middle adolescence. She's trying to figure out how to keep everybody happy.

* Burt is forty, overcommitted and undercommunicative.

* Celeste is forty and just about fed up.

* Chip is twenty and in charge of getting his own way.

Meet The Fines

FADE UP. A FIGHT IS UNDERWAY

> **CELESTE**
> (angry)

Fine!

> **BURT**
> (sarcastic)

Fine!

BURT HIDES BEHIND A NEWSPAPER

> **NICOLE**
> (overeager)
> Mama! I don't **have** to choose. It was
> just a suggestion. Pizza is fine.

> **CHIP**
> (enthusiastic)

Fine!

> **CELESTE**
> Hush, Chip, it's your **sister's** birthday.
> Tell him to be quiet, Burt.

BURT LOOKS OVER HIS PAPER

> **BURT**
> You heard your mother…

> **CELESTE**
> I don't know why we can't just think
> about someone besides **ourselves**
> around here.

NICOLE
Mama!

CELESTE
Oh, baby, I don't mean you. But I **do**
mean the **rest** of us.

CHIP
If we don't eat soon, I'm gonna pass out.

CELESTE
Oh, like you did something other than
lay around all day.

CELESTE STORMS OFFSTAGE SHOUTING

Speak to your son!

COMING FROM BEHIND HIS NEWSPAPER, BURT GIVES CHIP A LOOK
AND LEAVES THE ROOM IN THE OTHER DIRECTION, GRUMBLING AS
HE GOES

BURT
You heard your mother, Chip.

NICOLE TURNS TO ADDRESS THE AUDIENCE

NICOLE
I can't believe this. Can we just stop
fighting for five minutes so we can pick
a place to eat?

CHIP CROWDS NICOLE AS HE CROSSES THE STAGE TO EXIT AND SHE
ADDRESSES HIM

Why are you so mean to me, Chip? I
wish you'd just go back to college or get
a job or just, just, go *away*!

CHIP
(mocking)
Why are you so mean to me, Chip!

Drop dead, Birthday Girl.

CHIP EXITS AFTER HIS FATHER AND NICOLE ADDRESSES
THE AUDIENCE

NICOLE
I *knew* this would happen. It always
does.

I am so lame!

VOICE OFFSTAGE
Why are *you* lame? Doesn't Chip get to
pick the restaurant on his birthday?

NICOLE
[matter of factly]
He picks for *everybody's* birthday.

VOICE OFFSTAGE
And that's OK with you?

NICOLE
Well…no. It's not *OK*…but it's not a big
deal either. I mean, it's a stupid restaurant.

VOICE OFFSTAGE
Why am I not convinced?

NICOLE
[irritated]
Why are you even *here*?

VOICE OFFSTAGE
Don't ask silly questions. The real question is, Why is *Chip* here?

NICOLE
Don't get me started on Chip.

VOICE OFFSTAGE
Too late. Didn't he already leave once?

NICOLE
He did, but he came back.

VOICE OFFSTAGE
To *work*.

NICOLE
Supposedly. He doesn't even leave the house until after dark.

VOICE OFFSTAGE
But then, he doesn't come home until dawn…

NICOLE
I wouldn't know.

VOICE OFFSTAGE
Wouldn't you?

NICOLE TURNS AND SHOUTS

NICOLE
You guys! Are we going? I've decided I want pizza!

THE OTHERS ENTER

CHIP
Cool!

CELESTE
[harsh]

Be quiet, Chip.

[sweetly]
Are you sure honey? It's your birthday…

NICOLE
I'm sure, Mama. Can we just go.

AS THEY APPROACH THE DOOR, THE DOORBELL RINGS. BURT ANSWERS. A MAN IN KHAKI WITH A SHOVEL AND A BIG BAG IS THERE

MAN
Somebody call about removing some elephant droppings?

EVERYONE LOOKS ASTOUNDED.

EACH ONE SPEAKS OVERLOUD FOR EFFECT, THEN WHISPERS TO THE MAN AS THEY BRUSH PAST THE MAN AND EXIT.

BURT
What the… You got the wrong house buddy! (Where *were* you? I thought you were coming *yesterday*.)

CELESTE
For *goodness* sake! (*Try* not to get any on the sofa this time.)

CHIP
Pachyderm Poop! This place is nuts. I gotta get an apartment! (Touch my Gameboy and I'll have you killed.)

NICOLE
I have no idea what you're talking about. (The worst of it is in the living room.)

[deadpan to the audience]

I have no idea what he's talking about.

BURT (OFFSTAGE)
You coming! We're gonna leave you!

NICOLE
(angry)
Fine!

TO BLACK

Rinse The Blood Off My Toga

Rinse the Blood Off My Toga is so old that its origins are lost in the fog of time. The earliest recorded performances date to the inter-Testamental period and it is said that the Apostles performed *Toga* at camp one summer.

My revision—some would say perversion—of Toga was done to update it and make it into a five-part series for our weekly senior high meeting. You can use it for camp or, if you can stomach it, do it all at once. If you still love the original, I don't know what you'll think of my tinkering with it. In truth, if you still love the original you're very old and probably can't see to read this anyway.

SYNOPSIS

Gluteus Maximus, a private detective in ancient Rome, tries to solve the murder of Julius Caesar. *Rinse the Blood Off My Toga* is here revised as five episodes, each running fivish minutes.

NOTES

* A few sound effects will go a long way in this show. The sound effects person or persons could even be in plain sight if you want to add to the fun.
* The Announcer talks like the announcer on the *David Letterman* show.
* Gluteus Maximus has a HUGE butt and talks like Maxwell Smart.
* Citronella has a New York accent.
* Brutus is menacing.
* Calpurnia is a hysterical Southern woman.
* Mark Antony is sleazy.
* Claudius is your basic bartender type.
* The Senators are a Greek chorus.
* Wrap everybody in sheets. Flowers and plaids? It just doesn't matter.

Rinse the Blood Off My Toga

Episode One

ANNOUNCER

The Scene: Imperial Rome. The year: I
forget exactly—but a long, long time
ago. One man stands out from the
crowd. He is Gluteus Maximus.

GLUTEUS MAKES HIS ENTRANCE IN PROFILE. HE ADDRESSES THE
AUDIENCE AND FLASHES HIS BADGE AT THE APPROPRIATE MOMENT.

GLUTEUS

The name's Maximus—Gluteus
Maximus, Private Eye. I carry a shield.
Rome is my beat. I'm just an honest guy,
trying to make an honest drachma. It's
not easy.

I've walked this beat for twenty years.
Now I drive a chariot. My license number? IXIVLLCDIXMVI. Also comes in
handy as an eye chart. My social security num…Sorry: I'm getting carried
away. You're easy to talk to.

Tonight I'll tell you about the Julius
Caesar caper.

It was the Ides of March. I'd just sent
another criminal up the Tiber—Sutonius,
the Gladiator. He was fixing fights at the
Coliseum. Had a rubber sword scam
going but I helped him get the point.

Now, back in my office, I wasn't surprised when my associate, Citronella,
walked in.

ENTERING, CITRONELLA TOSSES MARBLE POSTCARDS. THEY
CRASH.

CITRONELLA
Morning, Gluteus, I picked up the mail.

GLUTEUS
Easy with those postcards, doll. You
could break my legs. What's shakin'?

CITRONELLA
That fatty tissue underneath your arms.

GLUTEUS
Ooh!

CITRONELLA
Oh, and there's somebody outside to see
you. Seems awfully excited.

GLUTEUS
O.K., send him in.

CITRONELLA
With all due respect, Gluteus, gettim
yerself.

GLUTEUS
Would you come in, sir?

BRUTUS ENTERS

BRUTUS
Thanks, Toots. You Maximus?

CITRONELLA GRABS BRUTUS BY THE TOGA

CITRONELLA
That's **Ms**. Toots to you.

CITRONELLA EXITS AS GLUTEUS SPEAKS

BRUTUS
Sure…Ms. Doll.

GLUTEUS
Easy, Nell; he don't mean nothin by it.
I'm Maximus. What's on your mind?

BRUTUS
Are you sure we're alone?

GLUTEUS
I'm sure we're alone.

BRUTUS
Well, who's that standing beside you?

GLUTEUS
That's you.

(to audience)
I could see I was dealing with no
ordinary man.

BRUTUS
Maximus, a terrible thing has happened.
It's the greatest crime in the history of
Rome.

GLUTEUS
I'll be the judge of that. Give it to me
straight.

CITRONELLA REENTERS AS BRUTUS DELIVERS THE LINE

BRUTUS
Julius Caesar has been murdered!

NELL AND GLUTEUS REGISTER SHOCK AND FREEZE FOR A MOMENT

GLUTEUS
(to audience)
Caesar murdered! I couldn't believe my
ears. Big Juli, dead!

BRUTUS
He was killed just twenty minutes ago.
It happened in the Senate. He was
stabbed.

GLUTEUS
Stabbed! No!

BRUTUS
They got him in the rotunda!

GLUTEUS
Oh, that's **so** painful. I got a splinter
there one time; *very* tender.

BRUTUS
I tell you, Maximus, all of Rome is in an
uproar. I came to you because you're the
best. You've got to find the killer.

GLUTEUS
[flattered]
Well, I'll try.

BRUTUS
You can do it! You're the one who sent
Nero up on that arson rap.

GLUTEUS
Oh yeah, well, Nero. The whole
town was pretty burnt up about that,
eh? (Laughs) Get it? Whole town? Burnt
up? By Jupiter! Sometimes I just slay
myself!

BRUTUS
What do you say, Maximus? Will you
take the case?

ALL FREEZE AND THE ANNOUNCER STEPS IN

ANNOUNCER
Will Maximus take the case? Will
Citronella find her place in the world?
Will Brutus outlive the Popeye jokes?
Tune in next week as we hear Gluteus
Maximus say:

GLUTEUS
Are we finished?

TO BLACK

Rinse the Blood Off My Toga

Episode Two

ANNOUNCER COMES ON AND EACH CHARACTER ENTERS AS HE OR SHE IS INTRODUCED

> **ANNOUNCER**
> In our last episode, Gluteus Maximus, Private Eye, was approached by a mysterious stranger who turned out to be none other than his erstwhile associate, Citronella.
>
> You may be thinking, "No one could be stranger than Citronella," but you'd only be half right. Then again, you'd be half wrong. And so it should come as no surprise—especially if you saw the last episode—which was really the first episode—we're a *long* way from the last episode, if you know what I mean. In any event, Gluteus and Citronella were approached by yet another—stranger still—called Brutus, who came with the news that Caesar was dead—stabbed in the rotunda.

ALL WINCE

> **BRUTUS**
> What do you say, Maximus? Will you take the case?

> **GLUTEUS**
> (suspicious)
> Just a minute, Bub. Who's askin'? I like to know who I'm working for.

BRUTUS
Name's Brutus. I'm a senator. I was
Caesar's best friend.

GLUTEUS
A Senator! Very impressive. And with
friends. Very…unusual.

All right, Brutus, you got yourself a boy.
My fee is 200 drachmas a day—payable
in advance; *plus* expenses.

BRUTUS
Done, Maximus.

BRUTUS POURS COINS IN GLUTEUS'S HAND

GLUTEUS
Just a minute, Brutus. You're one short.

BRUTUS
Hey, you got a good ear.

GLUTEUS
When it comes to money, perfect pitch.

BRUTUS EXITS AND GLUTEUS COMES TO THE EDGE OF THE STAGE
TO CONFIDE IN THE AUDIENCE. CITRONELLA TRIES TO INTERRUPT
WHILE HE ADDLES ON.

GLUTEUS	**CITRONELLA**
(to audience)	Max, some of us have *school*
We took my chariot to the	tomorrow.
Via Appia. The streets were	
crowded with the usual	
suspects—slaves, legion-	
naires, patricians, pickpock-	
ets, hookers, the rich, the	(insistently)
poor, the lame, the blind,	Uh, Gluteus, some of us have
hookers, people from out of	homework…
town, homeboys, people in	

search of a dream, people in search of a place to eat, people in search of a place to park, hookers, guys on bicycles, men dressed like women, sullen children and know-it-all adults, the best and the worst of humanity's teeming masses…

CITRONELLA
(shouting)
While we're young, Maximus!

GLUTEUS
[to Nell]
Sorry, they're easy to talk to.

[to the audience]
Before long we found ourselves at the Senate—where, as it turned out, the **real** trouble began.

BRUTUS
Well, Gluteus, this is where it happened. This is where Big Juli got it.

GLUTEUS
Hmmm. Where's the corpus delicti?

BRUTUS
The what?

GLUTEUS
The corpus delicti—the *stiff!* Don't you understand plain Latin?

BRUTUS
Oh, the *stiff.*

GLUTEUS
[rolling his eyes at the audience]
Oh, the stiff.

BRUTUS
Right over there.

GLUTEUS
Oo! Eight daggers.

BRUTUS
Yeah, what do you think?

GLUTEUS
I think if he were alive today he'd be a pretty sick boy!

BRUTUS
[injured]
Come on, Maximus; he was my friend. And he owed me a lotta dough. You gotta solve this crime.

GLUTEUS
He owed you a lotta dough? Awright, what's the funny business, Brutus?

BRUTUS
There's nothing funny about business, Maximus. We were about to franchise a whole new food line—called it "Little Caesar's." The deal fell apart. He got the ovens, but I never got the dough.

GLUTEUS
Awright, awright. Fill me in—who are those guys over there? The ones standing around doing nothing.

BRUTUS
Those are Senators. They were all here when it happened. There's Publius; and Sleazius; and that's Dufus.

GLUTEUS

Who's the on over there with the lean
and hungry look on his kisser?

BRUTUS

That's Cassius.

GLUTEUS

Looks like a loser from the Coliseum.
Which one do *you* think is the likeliest
suspect?

BRUTUS

I think it's the guy next to Cassius.

GLUTEUS

Wait a minute—that's *you*.

BRUTUS

Yes, but can I be trusted?

EVERYBODY FREEZES AND THE ANNOUNCER STEPS IN

ANNOUNCER

Can Brutus be trusted? Will we ever hear
from Citronella again?

How long can this go on?

Tune in next time, when we'll hear
Citronella say

CITRONELLA
[Three Stooges bit]
Oh, a wise guy, eh?...

71

Rinse the Blood Off My Toga

Episode Three

ANNOUNCER STEPS IN AND EACH CHARACTER ENTERS AS HE/SHE IS INTRODUCED

ANNOUNCER
In our last episode, the lovely and talented Citronella stood around while her
oppressive partner Gluteus Maximus,
Private Eye, hogged all the lines.

CITRONELLA
Watch yourself Maximus. Cross me and
I'll cut your butt down to size.

ANNOUNCER
Meanwhile, the ever-mysterious Brutus
became more inscrutable by the minute.

GLUTEUS
And who do *you* think is the likeliest
suspect?

BRUTUS
I think it's the guy next to Cassius.

GLUTEUS
Wait a minute—that's *you*.

BRUTUS
Yes, but can I be trusted?

ANNOUNCER
Join us now, as if you had any choice,
for Rinse The Blood Off My Toga,
Episode Three.

GLUTEUS
(to audience)
I could see I was dealing with no ordinary case.

SOUND OF FOOTSTEPS AND GLUTEUS CONTINUES

Yello! Who's the dame?

CITRONELLA
Wife of the deceased. Goes by the name, Calpurnia.

GLUTEUS
Yeah, well—she's a suspect.

Just a minute, Pardon me. Uh—Mrs. Caesar?

CALPURNIA
My husband's been murdered.
Whatever will I do now?

GLUTEUS
You could go to Disneyland. That's not legal advice, of course. Just a suggestion.

CALPURNIA
In France? Is that still open? Oh, I don't know…Those French people are so *rude*.

GLUTEUS
Never mind. Name's Gluteus Maximus, Private Eye. I'd like to ask you a few questions. What do you know about this?

CALPURNIA
(deep emotion, turns to hysteria)
I told him. I told him, "Juli, don't go."

GLUTEUS

What?

CALPURNIA

"Juli, don't go," I told him. But nooo, he wouldn't listen to me.

GLUTEUS

Now, look, Mrs. Caesar, I —

CALPURNIA

If I told him once, I told him a thousand times, "Juli, don't go..."

GLUTEUS

Don't get upset, ma'am —

CALPURNIA

I begged him, "Juli, don't go." I said, "It's the Ides of March. Beware." I said.

GLUTEUS

Yeah.

CALPURNIA

But does he listen to his wife? No! He's *Caesar*. Big deal.

And now he's...dead.

GLUTEUS

Awright, take it easy. You want to take care of Mrs. Caesar, Nell?

CITRONELLA

Come on honey. I'll take you home. *Great* sheet, where do you shop?

THEY EXIT STILL TALKING, GETTING FAINTER AS THEY GO

CALPURNIA

I told him, "Juli, don't go. Don't go," I said. But did he listen?

GLUTEUS
(to audience)
Who could blame him? All right, senators. You can go too, but don't leave town. And, hey: Do something about that deficit.

SENATORS GRUMBLE AS THEY LEAVE.

BRUTUS

So? What do you think?

GLUTEUS

I don't know! Not an angle anywhere. Not a clue. This is so per*plex*ing; so frustrating. I feel so stupid!

BRUTUS

Hey, easy big fella. Rome wasn't built in a day.

GLUTEUS

Wha'd you say?

BRUTUS

I said, "Easy big fella."

GLUTEUS

No, the other part.

BRUTUS

Rome wasn't built in a day?

GLUTEUS

That's good. "Rome wasn't built in a day." That's *very* good.

BRUTUS
You like it? It's yours.

GLUTEUS
Let's reconstruct the crime. Now, Caesar
was over there and—

BRUTUS
Right over here, yeah.

GLUTEUS
Shhh!

BRUTUS
What's the matter?

GLUTEUS
(softly)
Somebody's behind that statue.

BRUTUS
What statue?

A PLAYER SLIDES INTO THE SCENE AND FREEZES AS MARK
ANTONY SNEAKS BEHIND CARRYING A SACK.

GLUTEUS
That one right over there. Shush.
I'll go get him.

GLUTEUS JUMPS BEHIND THE STATUE AND GRABS MARK,
SHOUTING:

Awright buddy. Come on out. What are
you doin' hangin' around here?

MARK
Why shouldn't I? It's a free country.
Besides…I'm Mark Antony.

Maybe you caught my act at the Forum. It's a one man show, a tribute, really. Let me just give you a couple of pages—I'm poised over the body of Caesar and I say, "Friends, Romans, countrymen, lend me your ears—"

GLUTEUS
[cutting in]
Never mind the speech, what's in the sack?

MARK

Ears.

GLUTEUS

Get *away* from me!

MARK

Wait a minute. Don't you wanna know who bumped off Julius Caesar?

GLUTEUS

Wooden Eye!

MARK

Actually, it's lifelike *glass*. But that's not important now. The name of the murderer is: (dies in agony) ahh—ooooo—eeeee—- ohhhh—ahhhh.

GLUTEUS

Hmm... Must be *Greek*.

BRUTUS
Great Jupiter. He's dead!

GLUTEUS
(to audience)
What a case. All I got for clues is two dead bodies and a sackful of ears.

BRUTUS

Now, see here, Maximus—I'm paying
you one hundred eighty drachmas a day
to solve this case.

GLUTEUS

Two hundred.

BRUTUS

Sorry. That's right. You *do* have a good
ear.

GLUTEUS

I got a *sackful* of good ears.

BRUTUS

I'm losing patience, Maximus. I want
action!

GLUTEUS

Awright, awright. Don't get your toga in
a knot. Listen, I got a pal.

BRUTUS

Yeah?

GLUTEUS

Claudius. Runs a bar on the Via de la
Phlegm. He should have a few answers.

BRUTUS

That's the idea. Ask questions. Get out
among the people. Circulate. When in
Rome, do as the Romans do.

GLUTEUS

Hey—what was that again?

BRUTUS

Get out, cir—

GLUTEUS
[cutting in]
No, the last part!

BRUTUS
I said, "When in Rome, do as the
Romans do."

GLUTEUS
Oh—that's very good. "When in Rome,
do as the Romans do."

BRUTUS
You like that?

GLUTEUS
I love that!

BRUTUS
It's yours.

ALL FREEZE AS THE ANNOUNCER SPEAKS.

ANNOUNCER
Will Gluteus come up with anything?
Will Brutus get his toga in a knot? Will
somebody please tell me why I'm talking like this?

Tune in next week for more in the ongo-
ing saga of "Rinse The Blood Off My
Toga."

TO BLACK

Rinse the Blood Off My Toga

Episode Four

ANNOUNCER
In our last episode, Gluteus Maximus
watched as Mark Anthony died—

DISTANT SOUNDS OF MARK ANTHONY DYING

MARK
Oo; Ah; Ee!

ANNOUNCER
He listened as Caesar's wife, Calpurnia,
cried—

DISTANT SOUNDS OF CALPURNIA SHOUTING

CALPURNIA
I told him: Juli, don't go! Those were my
exact words!

ANNOUNCER
He *spoke* as Brutus pried—

DISTANT VOICES OF BRUTUS AND GLUTEUS

BRUTUS
I'm losing patience, Maximus. I want
action!

GLUTEUS
Awright, awright. Don't get your toga in
a knot.

ALL THE PLAYERS WALK ON STAGE AS THE ANNOUNCER
ANNOUNCES:

ANNOUNCER
Now it's time for Part Four of "Rinse the
Blood Off My Toga."

GLUTEUS
(to audience)
Claudius' bar is…Just a minute.
Claudius's bar is…I have such trouble
with words like that…The place where
Claudius serves drinks and food is a
hangout where I can always count on
getting some answers. It's a small place
with a few tables and a guy in the corner
playin' cool jazz.

CLAUDIUS
Hi ya, Glut.

GLUTEUS
Hi, Claud. What's new?

CLAUDIUS
Nothing much. What ya drinkin?

GLUTEUS
How about a martinus.

CLAUDIUS
You mean *martini*.

GLUTEUS
If I want two, I'll ask for 'em. Look, I'm
working on this Julius Caesar thing.
What have you heard?

CLAUDIUS
Try that dame over there.

GLUTEUS

Yeah?

CLAUDIUS

Yeah.

GLUTEUS CROSSES THE ROOM TO A WOMAN LOOKING THE OTHER WAY. WHEN SHE TURNS WE SEE THAT IT IS CALPURNIA.

GLUTEUS

Awright, sister, start talkin'. Hold the phone! It's *you*!

CALPURNIA

I told him, "Juli, don't go!"

GLUTEUS

Good grief!

CALPURNIA

"Juli, don't go..."

GLUTEUS

Get'er outa here! Hsheeee!

CLAUDIUS

Hey, look, uh—Gluteus. I, uh, think I might know the guy you're looking for.

GLUTEUS

You mean: Mr. Big?

CLAUDIUS

Mr. *Big*, El Honcho Grand, The Man, Numero Uno, the Head Cheese —

GLUTEUS

[cutting in]
Get on with it! We godda lotta ground to cover tonight!

CLAUDIUS

His name is: (dies in agony) ooooo—
eeeee—aaaaa—eeeeeeg.

GLUTEUS

It's that same *Greek guy*! Got a scroll,
Claud? I wanna write that name down.
Claudius? Claudius!

(to audience)
I would never get another martinus out
of him.

This was shapin' up bigger than I
thought. Suddenly I looked up. There
was Brutus.

BRUTUS

Hello, Gluteus.

GLUTEUS

Brutus, what are you doing here?

BRUTUS

I was lookin' for you. Who's that on the
floor?

GLUTEUS

Claudius, the bartender.

BRUTUS

Funny place to carry a knife—in his
back.

GLUTEUS

He's dead. He was stabbed—right
through the portico.

BRUTUS

Ooh, I hate that!

GLUTEUS
Tell me about it!

BRUTUS
You're running out of time, Maximus.
We've got to have answers. Who killed
Julius Caesar?

GLUTEUS
(to audience)
I started to think, and slowly the pieces
fell into place.

CRASHING NOISE

Brutus was the only man around when
all those guys were killed—Caesar,
Antony, the bartender—Brutus was
always there. Things were beginning to
add up. I put two and two together
came up with IV. It was time to make
my move!

BRUTUS
You came up with IV? You came up
with *Intravenous*?

GLUTEUS
I came up with four, stupid. Four stupid
dead ducks and that adds up to fowl
play: Caesar, Antony, Claudius…and
you, Brutus. You're the only one coulda
done it.

BRUTUS
Moi!?

GLUTEUS
Oui.

ALL FREEZE AS THE ANNOUNCER SPEAKS

ANNOUNCER
Will Gluteus solve the rest of the Julius
Caesar crime in French? Is Brutus Mr.
Big? Will the madness never cease?

Tune in next time when you'll see
Brutus do his impression of a duck:

BRUTUS DUCKS AS THE CAST ALL YELL

ALL
DUCK!

TO BLACK

Rinse the Blood Off My Toga

Episode Five

ANNOUNCER
In our last episode—wait a minute: THIS is our last episode!

Julius Caesar is dead along with a bunch of other people we hardly care about —

DISTANT SOUNDS OF PEOPLE DYING

ANNOUNCER
Juli's wife, Calpurnia, is an emotional wreck—

DISTANT SOUNDS OF CALPURNIA: "JULI, DON'T GO!"

ANNOUNCER
And Gluteus Maximus—the greatest private eye in the history of ancient Rome—is about to get his man!

GLUTEUS ENTERS WITH BRUTUS

GLUTEUS
Caesar, Antony, Claudius…and you, Brutus. You're the only one coulda done it.

BRUTUS
Moi!?

GLUTEUS
Oui. Let's not play games, Brutus. Or should I say—Mr. Big!
You knocked off Big Juli! If the sandal fits, wear it.

BRUTUS

Ha! You're out of your head. *I hired* you
to *find* the killer.

GLUTEUS

Smart, Senator. But not smart enough.
So: you gonna talk, or do I have to *lean*
on ya?

BLACKOUT, SOUNDS OF A STRUGGLE, THEN FADE UP

BRUTUS

All right, flatfoot. I did it. I admit it. I
knocked off Big Juli, and I'd do it again.

GLUTEUS

That's all I need. I'm sendin' you up the
Tiber for a long vacation. Tell him about
it, Nell.

NELL ENTERS

CITRONELLA

That's right, Brutus. You'll travel by boat
up the beautiful *Tiber River*.

Accompanied by the steady beat of gal-
ley drums, you'll row to *Northern Italy*
where you'll meet interesting people, get
plenty of exercise, AND it's *all expenses
paid*!

GLUTEUS

Come on down scum; I'm takin' ya in.

BRUTUS SLIPS BEHIND GLUTEUS

BRUTUS
One false move and you'll have a split
skirt, Maximus.

GLUTEUS
What the—

BRUTUS
I'm gettin' out of here. Don't try to stop
me!

GLUTEUS
(to audience)
He had the drop on me and I couldn't
stop him, but I knew where scum like
him would go:

The Senate—the scene of the crime.

FADE OUT & UP

GLUTEUS
Fifteen minutes later I pulled up in my
chariot. Hand me the ram's horn, Nell!

CITRONELLA
Got it, Glut.

GLUTEUS
(cups hands over mouth)
Awright Brutus. This is Gluteus
Maximus. I know you're in there. Come
out with your hands up!

BRUTUS
Come in and get me, flatfoot!

GLUTEUS
[to Nell]
How did he *know* about my feet! I can't
tell you anything.

CITRONELLA

I'm sorry. The man is very persuasive.
He's a Senator ya know…

GLUTEUS

There's no reason to be personal, Brutus.
Give yourself up. We can smoke you
out. We'll throw incense. We'll throw in
an onion on a spear!

BRUTUS

You can throw a party! I'm not comin'
out!

GLUTEUS

Awright, you asked for it! Let him have
it boys!

SOUND OF BREAKING GLASS, YELLING, GUNFIRE. LIGHTS BLINK.

BRUTUS EMERGES WITH HIS HANDS UP

GLUTEUS

Awright, Brutus, one false move and I'll
fill ya full of bronze!

BRUTUS

You got me, copper. But I'll be back!

GLUTEUS

Oh, no, you won't, creep. The gig is
over.

BRUTUS

What did you say? The *gig* is *over*? Don't
you mean the *jig* is *up*?

GLUTEUS

No, I don't mean the jig is up. I mean
this gig is over. It'll be years before we

do *Rinse The Blood Off My Toga* again.
You're finished.

BRUTUS
That's where you're wrong. I'll be back.
No matter what happens, no matter
where they send me, I'll find my way
back. "All roads lead to Rome."

CITRONELLA
Come on, you.

GLUTEUS
Wait, wait, wait! Bring him back!

BRUTUS
What?

GLUTEUS
That was a dandy!

BRUTUS
What are you talking about?

GLUTEUS
"All roads lead to Rome." That's *really*
good, you know that? You've got a gift
for this, Brutus, no kidding.

BRUTUS
You like that?

GLUTEUS
I *love* it!

BRUTUS
Well, you can't have it.

GLUTEUS
Get him outa here.

CITRONELLA
With pleasure.

SENATOR
Good work, Gluteus. All Rome salutes
you. Hail, Gluteus!

ALL
Hail, Gluteus!

GLUTEUS
Thanks, kids. There are just a few people
I'd like to thank…

Actually, if you don't mind, I've got a
date.

ALL
Whooo!

GLUTEUS
Ready sweetheart? You're sure your
husband doesn't mind.

CALPURNIA ENTERS AND THE TWO EXIT ARM IN ARM

CALPURNIA
Mind! I told him, "Juli, don't go…"

GLUTEUS
Good grief.

CALPURNIA
"Juli, don't go," I told him…

TO BLACK

The Boy

The Boy started out as a monologue. It was a sketch about how we see each other. What it grew into is a one act play about power and fear and the painful realization that there are no short cuts.

SYNOPSIS

Five people in a small town talk about a boy we'll never see. As they reminisce about The Boy, a painful story emerges. *The Boy* runs around thirteen minutes.

NOTES

* Mother and Father, Tom, and Coach are easy enough. I would tend to cast a woman as the Principal, though I suppose you could cast a man if you wish.

* They are in a void, standing in a semi-circle.

* At the beginning, they speak as if they were filling the audience in on a story they all know and we don't. After a while they forget about us and interact with each other.

* Tom doesn't enter until late in the act.

The Boy

AS THE LIGHTS COME UP, THE COACH, MOTHER, FATHER AND THE PRINCIPAL STAND IN A SEMI-CIRCLE. THEY SPEAK AS IF THEY WERE FILLING THE AUDIENCE IN ON A STORY THEY ALL KNOW AND WE DON'T. AFTER A WHILE THEY FORGET ABOUT US AND INTERACT WITH EACH OTHER.

COACH

The Boy was…mag*nificent*. No better way to say it. The kind of kid other boys fear. Not that he was exactly threatening, ya know. He was just so *above* everybody else. A nice enough kid. But still, you never knew…

PRINCIPAL

*Pain*fully handsome. His female teachers—the young ones—couldn't look The Boy in the eye. They were afraid he might read something there. Seventeen-year-old boys aren't supposed to be that finished. They just *aren't* that attractive to women. But there he sat, at the front of the class. More than just cute; disturbingly handsome.

The teachers had no desire to be five years younger. But The Boy showed up in more than one woman's dreams—five years *older* if you know what I mean.

MOTHER

He never dated—not much. I *think* for the same reason he didn't have many close friends. People were intimidated. They held back.

94

Asked me one time, "Mamma, what's wrong with me?" He thought he must be ugly—repulsive somehow to both boys and girls. He wondered why no one liked him.

FATHER

But that wasn't it. He was unapproachable, that's all. He seemed too good to be true, therefore, he must *be* too good to be true.

MOTHER

Course, The Boy knew none of this. What he knew was loneliness.

PRINCIPAL

No one was surprised when The Boy collected just about every sports honor a kid can get in high school.

COACH

Weren't surprised by the mob of recruiters that hounded his old man for a shot at selling their college program.

PRINCIPAL

It was *natural selection*, that's all. The *cream* rising.

FATHER

MVP as a sophomore; two years All-District, All-Region, All-State; honorable mention High School All-American as a junior and a pre-season pick as a senior.

MOTHER

And the letters; my word, the letters came from all over. And then phone calls and visits.

COACH

It's a wonder they even *found* Wilton. One-horse town...

FATHER

They *found* it.

PRINCIPAL

The Boy put us on the map.

FATHER

Guy calls from Texas: "We're in a rebuilding phase. You're just the kind of athlete we want to make our program into a national power. Let us bring you out to see the campus..."

'Nother one from Washington state says: "We're small, but you like that. This school'll fit like a glove. Listen, when can you come? We want you get a feel for what you can expect here..."

MOTHER

And the one from California: "We're about to get off probation with the NCAA. Year after next we'll be in a bowl game—ideal for a player like you." Like they *knew* him.

FATHER

Right. Guy says: "The best playing with the best, hey? Look, we want to fly you out here this weekend to meet some of the players and coaches..."

PRINCIPAL

It was like a movie, wasn't it— he was the star.

The People Who
Brought You This Book...

—— invite you to discover MORE valuable youth-ministry resources. ——

Youth Specialties offers an assortment of books, publications, tapes, and events, all designed to encourage and train youth workers and their kids. Just return this card, and we'll send you FREE information on our products and services.

Please send me the FREE Youth Specialties Catalog and information on upcoming Youth Specialties events.

Are you: ☐ An adult youth worker   ☐ A youth

Name _____

Church/Org. _____

Address _____

City_____ State ____ Zip _____

Phone Number (_____) _____

The People Who
Brought You This Book...

—— invite you to discover MORE valuable youth-ministry resources. ——

Youth Specialties offers an assortment of books, publications, tapes, and events, all designed to encourage and train youth workers and their kids. Just return this card, and we'll send you FREE information on our products and services.

Please send me the FREE Youth Specialties Catalog and information on upcoming Youth Specialties events.

Are you: ☐ An adult youth worker   ☐ A youth

Name _____

Church/Org. _____

Address _____

City_____ State ____ Zip _____

Phone Number (_____) _____

Call toll-free to order:

(800) 776-8008

BUSINESS REPLY MAIL
FIRST CLASS   PERMIT NO. 16   EL CAJON, CA

POSTAGE WILL BE PAID BY ADDRESSEE

YOUTH SPECIALTIES
1224 Greenfield Dr.
El Cajon, CA 92021-9989

Il.l.....l.lll.....l.l...lll.l.l.l.l.l.l.l.l......lll

Call toll-free to order:

(800) 776-8008

NO POSTAGE
NECESSARY
IF MAILED
IN THE
UNITED STATES

BUSINESS REPLY MAIL
FIRST CLASS   PERMIT NO. 16   EL CAJON, CA

POSTAGE WILL BE PAID BY ADDRESSEE

YOUTH SPECIALTIES
1224 Greenfield Dr.
El Cajon, CA 92021-9989

Il.l.....l.lll.....l.l...lll.l.l.l.l.l.l.l.l......lll

COACH
And everybody in Wilton had a supporting role.

MOTHER
We played the proud parents—

FATHER
[cutting in]
To perfection. Didn't just attend *games*. We went to The Boy's practices. Turned the garage into a weight room, didn't take a family vacation for—I don't know—

MOTHER
[cutting in]
Five years. The Boy had to go to sports camps. And his sister—sweet, talented, quiet…

PRINCIPAL
Best supporting actress. Walk through the part and never, ever upstage the Star…Is that right?

FATHER
[sadly]
That's right. I think we all understood.

COACH
Guys on the team took their cues from him—harmonized with him. They were grateful just to be on stage. I guess we all were.

PRINCIPAL
Wilton was dying. Everybody knew it and no one could do a thing about it.

FATHER

It was the *interstate* drew the
traffic away. We had nothing. No factory, nothing.

PRINCIPAL

It was so odd watching
Wilton turn into ghost town.

MOTHER

It was just a matter of time…

COACH

While we waited, the whole
town sort of adopted—

FATHER
[cutting in]
Nobody planned it.

COACH
[continuing]
Sort of adopted high school
athletics.

PRINCIPAL

We just woke up one day
and realized sports had
turned into our religion.

COACH

Sports in general—football
in particular.

PRINCIPAL

Which made The Boy a
prophet—

COACH
[cutting in]
Maybe even a kind of messiah.

FATHER
And you were high priest, Coach.

PRINCIPAL
And Friday night was church.

COACH
Whole town came down to the stadium
to see if The Boy would do a miracle.

FATHER
And the Saturday paper—forget about
it. It was the Gospel. Covered every
detail of Friday night.

COACH
Described it, told us what it meant,
praised it to high heaven.

PRINCIPAL
At least while The Boy was here.

COACH
That's how it was, everywhere and all
the time. We knew the end from the
beginning. The Boy could do no wrong.
Unless…

FATHER
Unless, God forbid, he got hurt.

MOTHER
All of us prayed against that.

COACH
No, that's right. If God was in his heav-
en, success *belonged* to The Boy.
Unless…

PRINCIPAL
Unless he forgot his lines. Unless he
missed his mark, tripped *himself* up, cru-
cified *himself*. But that could never happen—not in a million years. He knew
the script. He knew how it ended.
Unless…

COACH
Of all the bad advice he ever got—

FATHER
[cutting in]
Of which there was plenty.

COACH
Of which there was an a*bun*dance. Of all
that bad advice, I think only one piece
ever really *got* to The Boy.

It was off-season. One of those practices
that wasn't really a *practice* by the
strictest definition of the rules.

FATHER
To the casual observer it might *look* a lot
like practice.

COACH
But that would be a wrong observation
because off-season practices were unau-
thorized, see.

FATHER
Tom Corliss was home from college for
Spring Break.

PRINCIPAL
Tom was, himself, a hero before The
Boy's time. Went on to a highly respect-
ed football program.

COACH
I used to encourage Tom to come over
and mix with the kids whenever he was
home—

TOM ENTERS

TOM
Which I did—as much for my own ego
as for any love of the school. If I had let
myself think it, I would've been *glad* The
Boy played a different position than me.

COACH
You'd a been glad The Boy was enough
younger that you never had to share the
field with 'im.

TOM
I would. I guess if I'd let myself think
further I would've known that *I* felt iso-
lated in high school. So maybe he would
feel it even more.

PRINCIPAL
His talent was...

TOM
[finishing]
Bigger. And the town was smaller than
when I played.

But I *didn't* let myself think about it—
not exactly.

MOTHER
It was a thoughtless word that tripped
him up, Tom. Not malicious...thought-
less.

TOM

"Only thing I worry about," I told him, "is whether you're big enough to play with those guys. Those guys are *big*."

PRINCIPAL

"*How* big?" The Boy wanted to know.

TOM

"*Big!*" I said. "Bigger 'n you. You're gonna hafta put on some bulk. They'll kick yer butt."

COACH

Which was nonsense and he knew it. He was big and getting bigger. Put him to work with a real college trainer, he'd be unreal.

TOM

But I still said it. I was just trying to scare him.

COACH

Keep him in his place maybe? Keep him from gettin' cocky?

TOM

Maybe. It was stupid.

FATHER
At any rate, it was said. Slipped past
and it chilled him right to the bone.

MOTHER
For the first time since he was a little
boy, he wondered if he was good
enough.

COACH
Which terrified him, I think. He went
through a mean stage where he would
just take a kid's head off in practice.
Nobody called him on it or he might
take their head off.

PRINCIPAL
When a boy is lonely—when he's isolat-
ed from anyone who will really kid with
him, really tell him the truth, really find
out what's going on inside him—

FATHER
[cutting in]
When a boy is alone like that—

PRINCIPAL
A tiny seed of self doubt grows into a
redwood.

TOM
And what's he do then?

FATHER
What's The Boy do then…

MOTHER
He was a senior in college before he
knew he was sick.

COACH

Musta snuck around his body for most of *five* years before anybody had a clue.

TOM

Took him out in a matter of, what— *months*.

PRINCIPAL

Never saw anything like it. Read about it, you know…But never expected to *see* it.

FATHER

And the *thing* is…The thing *is* he was just so…*surprised* by the whole thing.

COACH

Never had a clue.

MOTHER

He was naive, really.

PRINCIPAL.

He should have learned it in class. We *taught* it.

TOM

He just didn't get it.

MOTHER

He thought that, because it wasn't *drugs* —

TOM
[cutting in]
In the traditional sense —

FATHER
[cutting in]
He thought that since it *wasn't* drugs in
that sense, it was OK…

COACH
He wasn't the only one.

MOTHER
He thought it was OK to—how do you
say it?

FATHER
He thought it was OK to shoot them
into his veins.

COACH
And since it was steroids, you know,
and not *drugs*, he just—they all just…

FATHER
He didn't get that it wasn't OK to share
the needle with the other guys. Never
even thought about it.

COACH
Never thought about it.

MOTHER
Well, he thought, "We're not drug
addicts, we're *athletes*."

PRINCIPAL
Should've learned it.

TOM
But he didn't.

FATHER
None of them did. Dumb jocks.

COACH
We lost six, seven boys from those two classes.

PRINCIPAL
Lucky it wasn't more, I guess.

MOTHER
They were so naive, really.

PRINCIPAL
Should've learned it…

FATHER
God, I miss him.

TO BLACK

Twelve Ways to Say No!

Twelve Ways to Say No! was written for a junior high school assembly. I don't think this piece stands alone because it begs the question *Do I really* want *to say no?* Nevertheless, *refusal skills* are important for everyone to learn—it's a part of learning to set healthy boundaries—and this little sketch is a fun way to introduce those skills.

Twelve Ways to Say No! is also an interesting way to introduce the idea that, for a lot of us, saying *no* to potentially harmful behavior is not a slam dunk. There's something else at work in us that makes *yes* a more plausible answer…

SYNOPSIS

Twelve light-hearted ways of saying *no* to risky behavior are demonstrated, culminating with a pie in the face. *Twelve Ways to Say No!* runs about a minute and a half.

NOTES

❋ You can perform *Twelve Ways to Say No!* with as many as thirteen characters and as few as two. Here, the players are numbered one through twelve.

❋ Everyone takes a half-step forward and addresses the audience.

❋ The most important elements are clarity and pace.

❋ Fill a pie tin with shaving cream or whipped cream.

❋ Put the pie in a paper bag and have each person pass it to the next after delivering the line. Or put it on a little cart or in a hat box that each person looks in or…

❋ When the pie is placed (not thrown; placing is funnier than throwing) turn the lights out as soon as the audience reacts.

Twelve Ways to Say No!

TWELVE
Twelve ways to say *no*.

ONE
[yelling]
No!

TWO
[sarcastic]
This is a joke, right?

THREE
Read my lips [mouth the word *No*]

FOUR
[Bronx Cheer]

FIVE
[annoyed]
Get serious.

SIX
[with a little of the evil eye]
I don't think so.

SEVEN
[country-fied]
When pigs fly!

EIGHT
[politely]
No thank you.

NINE
[laughter building to hysteria]

TEN
[knowingly]
You haven't heard, have you.

ELEVEN
[prissy]
I'm not that kind of boy!

TWELVE
[opens mouth to speak as Eleven places
pie in face]

Vows

Vows was written for a junior high school assembly. It's about the ultimate nature of addictive substances. It doesn't deal with addictive behaviors or relationships but it's a good introduction to the notion of addiction.

SYNOPSIS

Addiction asks kids to promise to follow through to the end on what they're beginning. Which is not quite what the kids had in mind. *Vows* runs about two minutes.

NOTES

❋ Cast are spread out downstage, facing the audience.

❋ Addiction speaks from upstage on a raised position. You can portray Addiction however you like: attractive, deathly, normal…you decide.

❋ Addiction interrupts each person "in the act." So, Marty is about to take a drink, Diane is about to smoke, and so on.

❋ Each player needs a handgun tucked out of sight.

Vows

MARTY IS ABOUT TO TAKE A DRINK.

ADDICTION
Before you take that sip: Will you drink every day?

MARTY
[surprised]
No. Just weekends…I guess. . .

DIANE IS ABOUT TO LIGHT A CIGARETTE.

ADDICTION
Before you take that puff: Will you find a way to get those every day? Will you bum them from friends; will you steal them if necessary?

DIANE
You must be joking. This is just something I want to do…I, ah, like the taste…I guess…

TERRY IS ABOUT TO SNORT WHITE POWDER OFF A SMALL MIRROR

ADDICTION
Hey! Before you snort that: Will you give up school; will you give up your family; will you give up everything you care about except the next line?

TERRY
What is this? I'm not giving up anything. This is for fun—because it *feels* good. This is for me. At least I guess it is…

GEN IS ABOUT TO LIGHT A PIPE OR A POP CAN BONG

ADDICTION
Before you light that: will you go on lighting it every day for the rest of your life, no matter how long—or how short—that might be?

GEN
If you're trying to scare me, don't bother. I know what I'm doing. You can't believe how this gets me up. And I've got friends who'll make sure I don't ever have to come down. These are people I trust. They wouldn't turn me on if it wasn't good, would they? I think not! They wouldn't, would they…

ADDICTION
Listen to me! You think this is a game…

You're right. It *is* a game. A little thing I like to call Russian Roulette. But it's worth the risk, right?

EVERYBODY LIFTS A GUN UNCERTAINLY TO HIS OR HER HEAD.

ALL
I guess so…

ADDICTION
[dead cold]
Guess again.

TO BLACK

You Think You're Alone

You Think You're Alone was written for a junior high school assembly. It's on the subject of *refusal skills*. Of course it's not the whole story and some in the audience will think it is pure propaganda if it is forced to stand alone. What it covers is *acting out*. What it doesn't cover is acting *in*. Acting in is just as big a problem as acting out but you'll never catch me doing it. I don't mean I won't act in, I mean you won't catch me.

By itself, *You Think You're Alone* could leave some people feeling defeated and some others feeling smug because they're clean so far as this list is concerned. Still, as part of a broader presentation, it's pretty effective.

SYNOPSIS

A kid confides to the audience that he or she has never really done any high-risk behaviors. A series of others offer reassurance that our speaker is not alone. *You Think You're Alone* runs about two minutes.

NOTES

❊ One is downstage center and addresses the audience.

❊ Gender doesn't matter.

❊ The other characters are upstage left and right. They address One.

❊ You can cast up to eight people, or as few as two or three.

❊ As the other characters speak, One looks out and over the audience as if making eye contact with someone behind us.

You Think You're Alone

ONE
Ok, ok: I admit it. I've never *been* drunk. Actually, I've never even had anything to drink.

I've never smoked. I've never gotten loaded.

I thought Crystal was somebody on television.

I thought LSD was the Mormons.

I've never…can I say this here? I've never had sex.

I've never thrown up to control my weight. I've never shoplifted.

I've never *done* **anything**!

So what does that make me—besides a virgin, I mean.

TWO
You think you're alone. But the number of people who smoke is dropping so fast it could make you dizzy. Face it: If it was ever cool to smoke, it's not now.

THREE
You think you're alone. But a *lot* of people—as many as half of us—never even *date* till after high school, much less have sex.

FOUR

You think you're alone. But most people don't use alcohol. I don't know where people get the idea that everybody is drinking. They must not get out much.

FIVE

You think you're alone. But the number of people using cocaine and crystal and LSD and even marijuana is pretty small.

Any is too many, but saying *everybody's* using is about as smart as saying all teenagers are obnoxious…

SIX

If you think you're the last sober, smoke-free, American virgin, relax.

SEVEN

Yeah: If you think you're alone, think again.

TO BLACK

Beautiful Dreamer

Beautiful Dreamer was written as Readers Theater for the opening night of a senior high summer camp. Joseph, the hero of the play, was the central figure in the week's small-group biblical content. We weren't confident that everyone was familiar with Joseph's story from the Book of Genesis. Hence, this embellished version of the story to get everyone on the same page.

Joseph's story is funny and encouraging in a scary sort of way. The encouragement is that God never, ever lets go and never, ever wastes pain. The scary part is that Joseph suffers a lot of pain spread over a long time. Can I trust a Person who works like that?

SYNOPSIS

Seventeen year-old Joseph is the apple of his father's eye and the pain in his brothers' collective neck.

The brothers fake his death and sell him into slavery. Years later, through miraculous acts of God and a whole lot of weird stuff, Joseph turns out to be the guy who saves Egypt from the effects of a grave famine. Coincidentally, he ends up saving his estranged family as well. *Beautiful Dreamer* runs around forty minutes.

NOTES

* Though this was written as Readers Theater, it would probably be even better as a play. [I suppose I'll get around to doing it that way eventually. In fact, I'd like to adapt it to the screen.]

* All the characters except Joseph and the Narrator are arranged like a Greek Chorus. Stagger them or put them on risers if you can.

* Use as many players as you can. The featured roles are the Narrator and Joseph. Supporting roles are Jacob, Reuben, Levi, Simeon, Judah, Potiphar, Potiphar's Wife, Pharoah's Baker, Pharoah's Cupbearer, Pharoah, and Joseph's Steward.

* The chorus is dressed in choir robes and, except for brief solo lines, step out to deliver their lines. People filling multiple roles might change hats, glasses, a feather boa for Potiphar's Wife, and so on.

* Gender is of little concern in the chorus—forget the names and have fun.

* Joseph should have a fine coat of many colors, but don't limit yourself to a bathrobe. Make it a letter jacket or a roadie jacket. Go nuts.

* Joseph is downstage center.

* The Narrator is downstage left.

* The Chorus is slightly upstage right.

* Longer solo lines—especially Potiphar's Wife—step out downstage right.

* Make up your own tune for Joseph's lament. Or call me and I'll hum you the one I made up.

Beautiful Dreamer

NARRATOR

Once upon a time, in a land far away, there lived an obnoxious seventeen-year-old named Joseph. It's not that he was unbelievably obnoxious—just that he was the youngest of twelve brothers…

CHORUS
[cutting in]

And one sister

NARRATOR

…and one sister, and spoiled rotten by their father and always talking loud and usually talking about himself. Unless, of course, he was talking about how lucky his brothers were to **be** his brothers.

JOSEPH

I had the most amazing dream last night. We were binding sheaves of grain out in the field, you see, when suddenly **my** sheaf rose and stood upright—this is so cool—while **your** sheaves gathered around mine and bowed down to it. Is that great or what?

CHORUS

Grrrr

JOSEPH

And **then** I had this other dream and this time the sun and moon and eleven stars were bowing down to me!

NARRATOR

Joseph's brothers had no trouble learning to hate him but their father, Jacob,
ate it up with a spoon.

JACOB

This kid; he kills me! Come over here,
boy. This dream you had: Will your
mother and I and your brothers **actually**
come and bow down to the ground
before you? Hoo, such spirit! Reuben,
did you hear what your little brother
said…

NARRATOR

And Joseph just kept pouring it on.

JOSEPH

But enough about me. What do **you**
guys think about me?

CHORUS

Don't ask.

NARRATOR

The old man gave Joseph a seriously
cool, if somewhat gaudy, jacket and they
both had to admit that he looked, not
just good, but really good. And Jacob
just couldn't get over how cute Joseph
was and neither could Joseph…

But Joseph's brothers were sick to **death**
of cute and they started looking for a
way to get rid of him.

LEVI

I'd like to smack that kid. You know
what I mean? Whatdaya think; should I
take him out?

SIMEON

No you can't **take him out**. This is delicate. It requires sensitivity and timing. I'm not saying you can't hurt him, but it's got to look like an accident.

LEVI

A **bad** accident? Can it look like a really bloody, painful, agonizingly-slow-death kind of accident?

SIMEON

Actually, that would be **nice**.

NARRATOR

And eventually they got their chance.

One day, while admiring how wonderful Joseph was, the boys' father said:

JACOB

You know who we haven't seen for a while is your brothers. I **sent** them someplace, didn't I? Where was that?

NARRATOR

And, of course, Joseph knew.

JOSEPH

That would be sheepherding, Dad. You sent them out to herd sheep at Shechem.

NARRATOR

And, of course, his dad was overcome with the cleverness of the boy.

JACOB

I **love** this kid! Rachel, Honey, did you hear what Joey just did? He **remem**bered where the other boys are! Did I **tell** you this child is a genius from day one? Did I **tell** you…?

NARRATOR
And so it came to pass that the old man thought it would be a broadening experience for Joseph to visit his brothers in the fields—to see **why** a college education is so important. And he caused Rachel, his wife, to cause Dinah, Joseph's older sister, to cause Orpah, the woman who ran the kitchen, to cause Aaron, the kitchen boy who ended up actually doing the work, to make a huge lunch for his journey.

CHORUS
The kitchen boy is going on a journey?

SIMEON
No, **Joseph** is going on a journey to find the shepherds who are out in a field washing their socks by night when an angel of the LORD appears to them and they are shore afraid.

NARRATOR
No, sorry. Wrong shepherds, wrong Joseph, wrong story. **Our** Joseph is going to check up on his sheep-herding brothers and bring word back to his dad who can't get over how cute he is. But **really** he's going to give his brothers the chance they've been looking for. They don't know it, he doesn't know it, but **Someone** knows…

So Joseph wandered round the countryside until, in due course, he came in sight of his brothers—which is to say they saw him before he saw them.

LEVI

Argh! It's that little son of a female dog,
wolf or fox coming out here dressed for
a stinkin' **pep** rally. I **hate** that kid,
Reuben. Let me take a shot at him,
wouldja? Let me nail his hiney!

NARRATOR

But Reuben stopped him because he saw
a bigger picture and, though it wasn't
the biggest picture, it was enough to
keep our story rolling.

JOSEPH

Hi guys! Dad says hi, Mom says hi,
Dinah says hi, Leah says hi, Zilpah says
hi, everybody says hi.

Say, do you notice a strong odor out
here, or is it just me? Whoa, it's **you**!
Hoo! It must be **nasty** in those sleeping
bags!

So what're you guys up to?

CHORUS

Don't ask.

NARRATOR

And Joseph's smelly, nasty, unscrupu-
lous brothers grabbed him and smacked
him around and threw him in a dry well
till they could think up more ways to
smack him around.

And Joseph was stunned and confused
and deeply hurt.

JOSEPH

And I was stunned and confused and
deeply hurt and I cried out to the LORD.

NARRATOR
That's right, baby, let it out, you cried
out to the LORD…

JOSEPH
I said, "Help me, Jesus!"

CHORUS
That's right!

JOSEPH
I said, "Help me in my moment of
need!"

CHORUS
Yes he did!

JOSEPH
I said, "Help me when I'm down!"

[CHORUS IMPROVISES AFTER EACH LINE FROM JOSEPH.]

JOSEPH
Help me when I'm out!

Help me when I'm misunderstood!

Help me when men say all manner of
evil against me!

Help me when I'm alone and afraid!

Help me in the morning when I've cried
all night!

Help me in the evenin' when I'm weak
from a hunger I cain't quench.

Help me in the nighttime when I cain't
sleep for sorrow!

Help me when I'm so far down the only
way out is up!

Help me, Jesus!

Narrator
And Jesus did help Joseph. He helped
him sleep, he helped him dream, and he
helped him believe that he would help
him out.

Now the brothers were deeply divided
as to what to do with Joseph. One fac-
tion thought they should send his arms
East and his legs West and let his head
fall where it may. A good plan but not
perfect.

Levi
More pain!

Narrator
Others held that the old ways are best
and should be honored. They proposed
combining two classics.

Simeon
Let's do the burying-up-to-the-neck-in-
sand for a couple of days and then finish
with the ants-and-honey-on-the-head
thing. It could be quite elegant, really.

Narrator
But Judah, partly because he loved his
father and partly because he loved a
buck and perhaps just a smidgen
because he thought Joseph wasn't **that**
bad, and maybe a tad because he was
afraid of God, proposed to sell the boy
and buy some beer.

And that, more or less, is what they did.

So Joseph found himself strapped to the southside of a westbound camel and calling out to his brothers:

JOSEPH
This isn't funny you guys! I'm tellin'! Daddy's really gonna be mad! Guys!

NARRATOR
But his brothers turned up the music and drank faster and shredded his seriously cool, if somewhat gaudy, jacket and dipped it in goat's blood and tried not to think about what their father was going to do when they got home.

And as he disappeared over the horizon, Joseph began to develop a genuine dislike for camels.

JOSEPH
So, where we going, you guys?

CHORUS
Don't ask.

• • •

NARRATOR
There was a time, now long gone, when Egypt was a good deal more pleasant than it is today. It was a time when the north-flowing Nile overflowed with prosperity, a time of burgeoning agriculture, a time when tourists wore **robes** and knee socks were not allowed with sandals.

It was to this Egypt that Joseph came
and was sold into the service of one
Potiphar, a heavyweight in the court of
the great Pharoah.

It turned out to be a heck of a buy for
Potiphar because the LORD was with
Joseph and he prospered. When
Potiphar saw that the LORD gave
Joseph success in everything he did, he
thought:

POTIPHAR
There's something about this kid. I'm
thinking he got serious potential as a
personal assistant. Hey, can somebody
get me a sandwich, thank-ewe.

NARRATOR
And the personal assistant thing worked
out very nicely.

POTIPHAR
I'm thinking I might just put him in
charge of the household—you know, let
him take care of everything I own. I
know he's only 18, but there's something about this kid. Hey! I'm waiting
out here! Are you bringing those chips
or what!

NARRATOR
And from the time he put Joseph in
charge, the LORD blessed the household
of the Egyptian because of Joseph. The
blessing of the LORD was on everything
Potiphar had and with Joseph in charge,
he did not concern himself with anything except the food he ate. Which was
a lot.

Did we mention that Joseph was well-built and handsome? Well, he was and after a while his master's wife, who shall remain nameless, took notice of Joseph and said:

WIFE
Come to bed with me!

CHORUS
Whooo!

NARRATOR
But the kid—having a great deal of class—refused nobly.

JOSEPH
Milady, please. With me in charge my master concerns himself with nothing except what he eats, which is plenty. Everything he owns he has entrusted to my care.

No one is greater in this house than I am. He has withheld nothing from me except you, because you are his wife. How then could I do such a wicked thing and sin against God? No way! Huh-uh, forget about it, I'm not that kind of boy, you're a nice lady and all but this is not gonna happen—is it hot in here or is it just me—so just you get it out of your mind, understand? Ma'am? Lady? Are you still there?

NARRATOR
Of course she **was** still there and she kept at it. But though she spoke to Joseph day after day, he refused to go to bed with her or even be with her.

One day he went into the house to attend to his duties, and none of the household servants was inside.

CHORUS

Uh-oh.

NARRATOR

And Potiphar's wife snuck up on him.

CHORUS

Holey moley, kid! Watch out!

NARRATOR

But it was too late. She caught him by his robe and said:

WIFE

I'm telling you for the last time, Joe: the gods have ordained it.

I've got breasts like the pyramids, and legs like the Nile. My hips sway like the palm trees and—catch this—my eyes are limpid pools. I'm soft as a lamb and hungry as a lion. I'm more woman than you've ever dreamed of! Now **come** to bed!

NARRATOR

But he didn't. He squirmed and wiggled and left her holding his empty robe while he ran like the wind.

When she realized she'd lost him again, she was so mad that she looked at the robe in her hand and she looked at his cute tush heading for the hills and it just made her mad and she screamed bloody murder.

WIFE

Ahhhhh! Wouldja look at this! This Jew has come in here to make us look like fools! He snuck in here to sleep with me—in the middle of the day, I might add—but, of course, I screamed. Well it's a good thing I did. He left his robe right here beside me and ran out of the house buck naked. Ohhh, I think I'm going to faint.

NARRATOR

And then it was too late to back out. When Potiphar came home, she told him the whole, sordid, flourishing falsehood.

And Potiphar was peeved.

Joseph, always thinking the best, came out of hiding when the boss returned, sure he would get a fair hearing. But he was wrong. Potiphar put him in the deep, dark, dank, dreary dungeon where the king's prisoners were held.

And Joseph was stunned and confused and deeply hurt.

JOSEPH

And I cried out to the LORD!

CHORUS

That's right, he cried out to the LORD.

JOSEPH

I said, "Help me, Jesus in my time of need!"

CHORUS

Help me, Jesus in my time of need!

UNISON
Listen to the words of my prayer

Help me, cause I know you are there

JOSEPH
You pulled me out of the hole

CHORUS
You pulled him out of the ground

JOSEPH
I know You saved my soul

CHORUS
When there no one around

UNISON
If you could do it then

Please could you do it again

JOSEPH
You got to help me, Jesus

CHORUS
Got to help him, LORD

JOSEPH
You got to help me, Jesus

CHORUS
Got to help him, LORD

JOSEPH
Sha da da bop, bood'n bod'n dood'n
daad'n do-*wow!*

• • •

NARRATOR

While Joseph was in prison, the LORD
did help him; he showed him kindness
and granted him favor in the eyes of the
prison warden so that he was put in
charge of all those held in the prison,
and made responsible for all that was
done there. The warden paid no attention to anything under Joseph's care,
because the LORD was with Joseph and
gave him success in whatever he did.

Time passed slowly till, one day, the
great Pharaoh had a hissy fit with the
head caterers which led to drastic mea-
sures. He had them taken into custody
by the captain of the guard which, if
you've paid attention you realize, land-
ed them in the same fix as our hero.
And it was to none **other** that the captain of the guard assigned them, and he
attended them.

CHORUS

Joseph was put in charge of the
Pharoah's cupbearer and baker?

NARRATOR

Precisely.

Time passed slowly some more until one
night when each of the two men—the
cupbearer and the baker—had one
dream each on the same night, and each
dream had a meaning of its own. Are
you with me?

JOSEPH

Why so glum kids?

Cupbearer and Baker
We both had dreams and we have no idea what they mean.

Joseph
No surprise there. I believe The Lord is in charge of that department. Tell me more.

Cupbearer
In my dream I saw a vine in front of me, and on the vine were three branches. As soon as it budded, it blossomed, and its clusters ripened into grapes. Pharaoh's cup was in my hand, and I took the grapes, squeezed them into Pharaoh's cup and put the cup in his hand.

Joseph
Cool dream. What it means is: The three branches are three days. Within three days Pharaoh will lift up your head and give you your old job back and everything will be just like before. But, hey, don't forget about **me**, wouldja? Mention me to Pharaoh and get me out of this place. I was kidnapped and carried off from the land of the Hebrews, and even here I have done nothing to deserve being put in a dungeon. I don't wanna whine but I'm a little sick of it.

Narrator
When the chief baker saw that Joseph had given a favorable interpretation, he said:

Baker
I too had a dream: On my head were three baskets of bread. In the top basket were all kinds of baked goods for

Pharaoh, but the birds were eating them out of the basket on my head. So what's it mean?

JOSEPH
Don't ask.

NARRATOR
And he wished he hadn't. Joseph said that within three days his head would also be lifted up—and **cut off**—and hung on a tree for the birds to munch.

CHORUS
Bummer.

NARRATOR
Yeah. Well anyway, the third day was Pharaoh's birthday, and he threw a huge party for himself. It will be no surprise to you that everything happened as Joseph had predicted. The birds were pretty happy with the outcome, as was the Cupbearer. **He** was so happy that he bore the cup not only for Pharoah but a couple of dozen times for himself as well and plum forgot to remember Joseph.

CHORUS
Bummer.

NARRATOR
Yeah. And **two years** passed.

CHORUS
Major bummer.

NARRATOR
That's right, I said two full years passed

and one night, in the dark of the middle
of the night, when not a creature was
stirring, *Pharaoh* had a dream.

CUPBEARER

Morning, your greatness. **Saay**, master:
why so melancholy, baby?

PHAROAH

Uhm…Dreams, my cupbearing inferior.
Deep, sober, bewildering dreams.

CUPBEARER

Well. Nothing a cup of this won't fix.
Cream?

PHAROAH

Magicians.

NARRATOR

And the magicians and wise men came
to Pharoah and heard his dreams but
could only suggest that perhaps late-
night snacks were not such a good idea
for a monarch of his age.

But the cupbearer smacked himself on
the forehead and said:

CUPBEARER

You know, your coolness, I was just
remembering that time when you got a
little out of sorts with a couple of us just
before your birthday and—boy I feel like
such a Big Silly—but, you know, me and
the Baker had these dreams while we
were…on **vacation**, and—stop me if
you've already heard this—there was
this young Jewish kid working in
the…**resort**, and we told him our
dreams, and he told us what they meant,

and things turned out exactly like he said: I got my job back—and may I say, sir, what a privilege it's been to serve you—and the Baker, ah…took a new, ah…somewhat **higher** position.

Now whatdaya think are the chances that I'd remember that on this particular day? (Oh God please let the kid still be there!)

NARRATOR

And, of course, he was. And Pharaoh sent for Joseph, and when he had shaved and changed his clothes, he came before Pharaoh.

PHAROAH

Let me get to the point, kid. I had a dream, and no one has any idea what it means. The word on the street is you can help with this sort of thing.

JOSEPH

Ooh, sorry, no can do.

PHAROAH

Guards!

JOSEPH

God, however, will give Pharaoh the answer he desires.

NARRATOR

Then Pharaoh said to Joseph:

PHAROAH

In my dream I was standing on the bank of the Nile, when out of the river there came up seven cows, fat and sleek, and they grazed among the reeds. After

them, seven other cows came up—
scrawny and very ugly and lean. I had
never seen such ugly cows in all the
land of Egypt. The lean, ugly cows ate
up the seven fat cows that came up first.
But even after they ate them, no one
could tell that they had done so; they
looked just as ugly as before. Then I
woke up.

JOSEPH

And…

PHAROAH

And, it was a dream. And then I had
another just a bad as the first. I saw
seven heads of grain, full and good,
growing on a single stalk. After them,
seven other heads sprouted—withered
and thin and scorched by the east wind.
The thin heads of grain swallowed up
the seven good heads. It was terrifying. I
told this to the magicians, but none
could explain it to me.

JOSEPH

I see…Well. It's like this: The dreams of
Pharaoh are one and the same. God has
revealed to Pharaoh what he is about to
do. The seven good cows are seven
years, and the seven good heads of grain
are seven years; it's same seven years,
get it? The seven lean, ugly cows that
came up afterward are also seven years,
as are the seven worthless heads of grain
scorched by the east wind.

PHAROAH

Am I missing something here?

JOSEPH

Feast and famine! Like I said: God has shown Pharaoh what he is about to do. Seven years of great abundance are coming throughout the land of Egypt, but seven years of famine will follow them. Then all the abundance in Egypt will be forgotten, and the famine will ravage the land. Everyone will forget the abundance because the famine will be so severe. The reason the dream was given to Pharaoh in two forms is that the matter has been firmly decided by God, and God will do it soon.

PHAROAH

And what is Pharoah supposed to do with this information?

JOSEPH

Well, if it were me, I'd look for a discerning and wise man and put him in charge of the land of Egypt. Then I'd appoint commissioners over the land to take a fifth of the harvest of Egypt during the seven years of abundance. They should collect all the food of these good years that are coming and store up the grain under the authority of Pharaoh, to be kept in the cities for food. This food should be held in reserve for the country, to be used during the seven years of famine that will come upon Egypt, so that the country may not be ruined by the famine.

That's what *I'd* do…if it were **me**.

PHAROAH

Well, my circumcised friend, it **is** you.

JOSEPH

Moi?

PHAROAH

Vous. Since God has made all this known to you, there is no one so discerning and wise as you. You shall be in charge of my palace, and all my people are to submit to your orders. Only with respect to the throne will I be greater than you.

I hereby put you in charge of the whole land of Egypt. I am Pharaoh, but without your word no one will lift hand or foot in all Egypt.

NARRATOR

Then Pharaoh took his signet ring from his finger and put it on Joseph's finger. He dressed him in clothes of fine linen and put a gold chain around his neck. He had him ride in a chariot as his second-in-command, and men shouted before him:

CHORUS

Outa tha way!

NARRATOR

Thus Pharoah put Joseph in charge of the whole land of Egypt when he was thirty years old and gave him an unpronounceable Egyptian name and the daughter of a prominent citizen to be his wife and Joseph went throughout the land of Egypt doing all the stuff he would do if he were in charge because now he were in charge.

For seven years Joseph stored up huge

quantities of grain, like the sand of the
sea; it was so much that he stopped
keeping records because nobody could
count that high.

Two sons were born to the happy couple
and Joseph named the first one
Manasseh and said:

JOSEPH
It is because God has made me forget all
my trouble and all my father's household.

NARRATOR
The second son he named Ephraim and
said:

JOSEPH
It is because God has made me fruitful
in the land of my suffering.

NARRATOR
Right on schedule, the seven years of
abundance in Egypt came to an end, and
the seven years of famine began, just like
Joseph said. And things were tough all
over, but in the whole land of Egypt
there was food.

When all Egypt began to feel the famine,
the people cried to Pharaoh who, in
turn, sent them to Joseph.

When the famine had spread over the
whole country, Joseph opened the store-
houses and sold grain to the Egyptians.
And folks came to Egypt from all over to
buy grain from Joseph, because the
famine was severe in all the world and,
of course, Joseph helped everybody out

because he was such a swell guy,
admired by all, and men ran ahead of
his chariot, shouting:

CHORUS
Outa tha way!

●●●

NARRATOR
Now, if this were a low-budget production we'd wrap it up about now and just
say, you know, something like: And
Joseph learned that it's a good thing to
endure suffering and all, and, you know:
When your life is in the pits Jesus will
help you out, you know and then we'd
close in prayer and all get to bed early or
maybe go out for pie or something.

But that is not the case. The story continues with a bizarre twist to an even more
useful conclusion, beginning back in the
old home town with Jacob and the boys.

REUBEN
What're you lookin at?

LEVI
I'm not lookin at anything, what're **you**
lookin at?

REUBEN
Stop lookin at me!

LEVI
Stop lookin at **me**!

JACOB
Why do you just keep looking at each
other? I have heard that there is grain in

Egypt. Go down there and buy some for us, so that we may live and not die.

NARRATOR
So ten of Joseph's brothers went down to buy grain from Egypt. But Jacob did not send Benjamin, the **new** youngest brother, because, after what happened to Joseph who knew where they might lose him?

Now Joseph was the governor of the land, the one who sold grain to all its people. So when the brothers arrived and bowed down to him, even with their faces to the ground, he recognized them. Of course they wouldn't have recognized him in a million years and he pretended to be a stranger and spoke harshly to them:

JOSEPH
You're not from around here, are you?!

NARRATOR
Stretched on the floor in front of him, their hineys in the air, Joseph's brothers told him they'd come from the land of Canaan to buy food. And he remembered his dreams about them and said to them:

JOSEPH
You are spies! You have come to see where our land is unprotected.

REUBEN
No, my LORD! Your servants have come to buy food. We are all the sons of one man. Your servants are honest men, not spies.

JOSEPH

No way! I have a sixth sense about this kind of thing. You have come to see where our land is unprotected.

LEVI

Your servants were twelve brothers, the sons of one man, who lives in the land of Canaan. The youngest is now with our father, and one is no more. And that's the truth.

JOSEPH

You lie like a dog! It is just as I told you: You are spies! And this is how you will be tested: As surely as Pharaoh lives, you will not leave this place unless your youngest brother comes here. You better get busy choosing someone to go home for him because the rest of you will be kept in prison, so that your words may be tested to see if you are telling the truth. If you are not, then as surely as Pharaoh lives, you are spies!

NARRATOR

And he put them all in custody for three days.

On the third day, Joseph said to them:

JOSEPH

Do this and you will live, for I fear God: If you are honest men, let one of your brothers stay here in prison, while the rest of you go and take grain back for your starving households. But you must bring your youngest brother to me, so that your words may be verified and that you may not die.

NARRATOR

And Judah said:

JUDAH

I knew this would happen! We're being punished because of what we did to Joseph. I told you we shouldn't have done it! We saw how bummed he was when he pleaded with us for his life, but did you listen? Noooo. That's why this is happening!

CHORUS

Shut up, Judah!

REUBEN

Did I tell you not to sin against the boy? I told you, but you wouldn't listen! Now we're gonna get it!

CHORUS

Shut **up**, Reuben!

NARRATOR

All of which might have been quite comical since Joseph was using an interpreter and his brothers didn't realize that he could understand them. But it wasn't all that funny because, as they talked, Joseph realized how much he loved them and turned away from them and began to weep. But then he got a grip and turned back and spoke to them again. He had Simeon taken from them and bound before their eyes.

Joseph gave orders to fill their bags with grain, to put each man's silver back in his sack, and to give them provisions for their journey. After this was done for them, they loaded their grain on their donkeys and left and travelled till nightfall.

JUDAH
Argh! Wouldja look at this! My silver is still in my bag! Oh man!

CHORUS
You're toast!

NARRATOR
But they all wondered, does God have a sick sense of humor or is he just mean?

When they came to their father Jacob in the land of Canaan, they told him all that had happened to them and that they had to take Benjamin to Egypt if they wanted to get Simeon back.

LEVI
Assuming you want Simeon back.

CHORUS
Shut up, Levi!

NARRATOR
As they were emptying their sacks, there in each man's sack was his pouch of silver! When they and their father saw the money pouches, they were frightened and cried with one voice:

CHORUS
We're toast!

JACOB
You have deprived me of my children. Joey is no more and Simeon is no more, and now you want to take Benjamin.

Everything is against me!

REUBEN
Dad, you can put both of **my** sons to death if I don't bring him back to you. Trust me, I'll bring Benjamin home.

JACOB
No way! I may have been born at night but I wasn't born **last** night. I got sons droppin' like flies. No way am I sending my Benjy down there. He's the first cute thing that's happened to this family in who knows how long and I'm not gonna risk it! Nosiree Robert! My son will **not** go down there with you. Don't think I don't see what you're up to. You're trying to kill me! With grief! Well you just fergit about it, boy!

• • •

NARRATOR
Now the famine was still severe in the land and Jacob had hardly finished his harangue before they had eaten all the grain they brought from Egypt.

JACOB
You better go back and buy us a little more food.

JUDAH
Dad, you're not gettin' it, are you? The man warned us solemnly:

JOSEPH
Don't come back without your brother.

JUDAH

If you send Benjamin along, we'll go down and buy food. But if you don't send him, we won't go because the man said to us:

JOSEPH

Don't come back without your brother.

JACOB

Why do you hate me? What did I do make you treat me this way? Why are you so unbelievably stupid? Did you have to tell the guy there was another brother?

LEVI

Dad, he tricked us! The man zeroed in on us with those beady Egyptian eyes and he wanted to know everything! "Is your father still living?" he asked us. "Do you have another brother?" he asked us. We just answered his questions. How were we to know he would say:

JOSEPH

Don't come back without your brother.

JUDAH

Let's get on with it, Dad. Send the boy and I'll guarantee his safety. If I don't bring him back you can hold me personally responsible; you can make me miserable for the rest of my life, OK?

Meanwhile, if we don't get out of here, you and we and our children will all starve while we talk about it! As it is, we could have gone and come back twice!

JACOB

You know, Judah, I would **never** have spoken to your grandfather in that tone of voice.

Do what you have to do but please, please, please, use just a little common sense. Pay the man the money you owe him. And take him some dates and maybe some honey…

And may God Almighty grant you mercy before the man so that he will let your other brother and Benjamin come back with you. As for me, if I am bereaved, I am bereaved.

NARRATOR

So the men took gifts and double the amount of silver **and** Benjamin and hurried down to Egypt to present themselves to Joseph. When Joseph saw Benjamin with them, he said quietly to the steward of his house:

JOSEPH

Take these men to my house and prepare dinner; they are to eat with me at noon.

NARRATOR

The brothers inquired as to what was to be done with them and the steward replied:

STEWARD

Don't ask…just kidding: My master is always saying that. Actually, you're going to his private residence. Who knows, we could be working together soon…just kidding!

NARRATOR
But the brothers weren't so sure, and
they looked at each other and said:

CHORUS
We're toast.

NARRATOR
But the Steward brought Simeon out to
them and took them into Joseph's house,
gave them water to wash their feet and
provided fodder for their donkeys. So
they prepared their gifts for Joseph's
arrival at noon and waited for what
seemed like a very long time.

• • •

When Joseph came home, his brothers
gave him the gifts and bowed down
before him to the ground. He asked
them how they were, and then he said:

JOSEPH
And how is your aged father you told
me about? Is he still living?

REUBEN
Your servant our father is still alive and
well.

NARRATOR
And they bowed low to pay him honor.

JOSEPH
And this is your youngest brother, the
one you told me about?

THE BROTHERS NOD AND PUSH BENJAMIN FORWARD A COUPLE OF
STEPS. BENJAMIN HALF BOWS, HALF CURTSIES, AND JOSEPH CON-
TINUES:

God be gracious to you, kiddo.

NARRATOR
At this point Joseph was so deeply
moved that he hurried out and went to
his private room where he cried like a
baby.

After he washed his face, he came out
and, controlling himself, had dinner
served.

They served him by himself, the brothers by themselves, and the Egyptians by
themselves, because Egyptians could not
eat with Hebrews, for that is detestable
to Egyptians. The men had been seated
before him in the order of their ages,
from the firstborn to the youngest; and
they looked at each other in astonish-
ment. When the meal was served from
Joseph's table, Benjamin's portion was
five times as much as anyone else's. So
they feasted and drank freely with him.

Now Joseph quietly gave these instruc-
tions to the steward of his house:

JOSEPH
Fill their sacks with as much food as
they can carry, and put each man's silver in the mouth of his sack. Then put
my silver cup in the mouth of the
youngest one's sack, along with the silver for his grain.

NARRATOR

As morning dawned, the men were sent on their way with their donkeys. They had not gone far from the city when Joseph sent his steward after them.

STEWARD

Why have you repaid good with evil? Isn't this the cup my master drinks from and also uses for magic? This is a wicked thing you have done.

JUDAH

No way! We even brought back the silver we found inside the mouths of our sacks the last time. So why would we steal silver or gold from your master's house? If any of your servants is found to have it, he will die; and the rest of us will become your slaves.

STEWARD

Very well, then, let it be as you say. Whoever is found to have it will become my slave; the rest of you will be free from blame.

NARRATOR

Each of them quickly lowered his sack to the ground and opened it. Then the steward proceeded to search, beginning with the oldest and ending with the youngest. And the cup was found in Benjamin's sack. At this, they tore their clothes and said:

CHORUS

Now we're really toast.

NARRATOR

Then they all loaded their donkeys and

returned to the city.

Joseph was still in the house when
Judah and his brothers came in, and
they threw themselves to the ground
before him. Joseph said to them:

JOSEPH
What is this you have done? Never
underestimate an Egyptian. Don't you
know that a man like me can find things
out by magic?

JUDAH
What can we say to my Lord? What can
we say? How can we prove our inno-
cence? God has uncovered your servants' guilt. We are now my LORD's
slaves—we ourselves and the one who
was found to have the cup.

JOSEPH
Please! Far be it from me to be so unfair!
Only the man who was found to have
the cup will become my slave. The rest
of you, go back to your father in peace.

JUDAH
Please, my LORD, let your servant speak
a word and don't be angry though you
are equal to Pharaoh himself. My Lord
asked his servants, "Do you have a
father or a brother?" And we answered,
"We have an aged father, and there is a
young son born to him in his old age.
His brother is dead, and he is the only
one of his mother's sons left, and his
father loves him."

Then you said to your servants, "Bring
him down to me so I can see him for

myself." And we said to my Lord, "The boy cannot leave his father; if he leaves him, his father will die." But you told your servants, "Don't come back without him." When we went back to your servant, my father, we told him what my Lord had said.

Then our father said, "Go back and buy a little more food." But we said, "We cannot go down. Only if our youngest brother is with us will we go."

Your servant, my father, said to us, "You know that my wife bore me two sons. One of them went away from me, and I said, 'He has surely been torn to pieces.' And I have not seen him since. If you take this one from me too and harm comes to him, you will bring my gray head down to the grave in misery."

So now, if the boy is not with us when I go back to your servant, my father, and if my father, your servant, whose life is closely bound up with the boy's life, sees that the boy isn't there, he will die. Your servant, that is to say *I*, guaranteed the boy's safety to my father. I said, "If I do not bring him back to you, I will bear the blame before you, my father, [your servant] all my life!"

Now then, please let your servant, I mean me, remain here as my Lord's slave in place of the boy, and let the boy return with his brothers. Just please, please, please don't make me face my old man without the kid.

NARRATOR

Then Joseph could control himself no longer:

JOSEPH

Everybody out!

NARRATOR

So there was no one with Joseph when he made himself known to his brothers. And he wept so loudly that the Egyptians heard him, and Pharaoh's household heard about it.

JOSEPH

I'm Joseph! Is my father still living?

NARRATOR

But his brothers were not able to answer him, because they were so freaked out. Then Joseph said to his brothers:

JOSEPH

Come close to me. It's me, your brother Joseph, the one you sold into Egypt! And now, don't be distressed and don't be angry with yourselves for selling me here, because it was to save lives that God sent me ahead of you. For two years there has been famine in the land, and for the next five years things will only get worse. But God sent me ahead of you to preserve for you a remnant on earth and to save your lives by a great deliverance.

So then, it was not you who sent me here, but God. He made me father to Pharaoh, LORD of his entire household and ruler of all Egypt. Now hurry back to my father and say to him, "This is what your son Joseph says: God has made me Lord of all Egypt. Come down to me; don't delay. You will live in the land of Goshen and be near me—you, your children and grandchildren, your flocks and herds, and all you have. I will provide for you there, because five years of famine are still to come. Otherwise you and your household and all who belong to you will become destitute."

You can see for yourselves, and so can my brother Benjamin, that it is really I who am speaking to you. Tell my father about all the honor accorded me in Egypt and about everything you have seen. And bring him here now!

NARRATOR
Then he threw his arms around his brother Benjamin and they cried like babies. And he kissed all his brothers and wept over them and they spent the rest of the day getting caught up.

When the news reached Pharaoh's palace that Joseph's brothers had come, Pharaoh and all his officials were pleased. Pharaoh said to Joseph:

PHAROAH
Tell your brothers, "Do this: Load your animals and return to the land of Canaan, and bring your father and your families back to me. I will give you the best of the land of Egypt and you can enjoy the fat of the land."

You are also directed to tell them, "Do this: Take some carts from Egypt for your children and your wives, and get

your father and come. Never mind
about your belongings, because the best
of all Egypt will be yours."

NARRATOR
So the sons of Jacob did this. Joseph
gave them carts, as Pharaoh had com-
manded, and he also gave them provisions for their journey. To each of them
he gave new clothing, but to Benjamin
he gave three hundred shekels of silver
and five sets of clothes. And this is what
he sent to his father: ten donkeys loaded
with the best things of Egypt, and ten
female donkeys loaded with grain and
bread and other provisions for his journey. Then he sent his brothers away, and
as they were leaving he said to them:

JOSEPH
And hey: No fighting!

NARRATOR
So they went up out of Egypt and came
to their father Jacob in the land of
Canaan. They told him:

REUBEN
Joseph is still alive! In fact, he is ruler of
all Egypt.

NARRATOR
Of course, Jacob was stunned at first and
didn't believe them. But when they told
him everything Joseph had said to them,
and when he saw the carts Joseph sent
to carry him back, the spirit of their
father Jacob revived. And he said:

JACOB

I'm convinced! My Joey is still alive! So pack already! If I'm gonna see him before I die we'd better shake a leg!

So, Reuben—from Day One—did I say this kid is genius or what?

TO BLACK

Christmas Dreams

Christmas Dreams was written as a Christmas pageant. It's a two-person show backed by a children's choir and the usual assortment of Angels, Shepherds, Wise Men, and the directors and parents of same. If you want to adapt *Christmas Dreams* to a narrower audience, you can replace the children with something more suitable. That might be slide and sound, or video, or an adolescent choir, or more group singing. In any event, I've left songs where they were in the first production.

SYNOPSIS

Joe and Maria are middle-aged folk preparing for another Christmas. Trouble is, Joe is so distracted by what's going on at work that he hasn't really thought about Christmas. Maria, on the other hand, is caught up in the details to the point that she may very well organize the meaning right out of Christmas. *Christmas Dreams* runs about half an hour, depending on the songs you choose.

NOTES

❊ The setting is Joe and Maria's family room. The Christmas tree is a work in progress. Joe sits in his favorite chair next to a floor lamp. Baby Joshua sleeps in a little cradle in the family room.

❊ Joe and Maria are stage right. The choir is upstage center. The stable is stage left.

Christmas Dreams

Scene One

EVENING IN JOE AND MARIA'S FAMILY ROOM.

MARIA IS DRESSING A CHRISTMAS TREE, BOXES SCATTERED AROUND HER.

JOE READS THE WALL STREET JOURNAL IN A CHAIR FLANKED BY A FLOOR LAMP AND A SMALL TABLE.

A DOORWAY, DOWNSTAGE RIGHT, LEADS TO BABY JOSHUA'S ROOM WHERE A CRADLE STANDS.

JOE FOLDS THE PAPER DOWN AND LOOKS OVER IT AT MARIA.

> **JOE**
> I found the perfect image for Christmas,
> Maria. It's a bunch of merchants gath-
> ered around a cash register —

> **MARIA**
> [cutting in]
> Joe, don't spoil this for me. If you can't
> help, at least don't spoil it for *me*.

> **JOE**
> No: this is great! You got a bunch of
> merchants gathered around a cash regis-
> ter and they're singing, "What a Friend
> We Have in Jesus!" Eh?

> **MARIA**
> Why do you always do this?

JOE GIVES MARIA A "WHO, ME?" GESTURE AND MARIA CONTINUES, EDGY.

You know exactly what I mean.

JOE

I don't even know *approximately* what
you mean. Why does this have to be an
ordeal every year?

MARIA

Joe…just leave it alone.

JOE
[from behind the paper]
Good advice, Maria.

MARIA

I'm sorry?

JOE

I said, "The tree looks nice."

MARIA

Do you think so? I think it needs another
string of lights. Would you run out and
pick up a string?

JOE FOLDS THE PAPER DOWN AGAIN AND PEERS OVER IT. HE PUTS
IT ASIDE.

JOE

No, Maria—see, it's fine. You always do
this. You just worry it to death.

MARIA

I want it to be right. Is that a problem?

JOE

It is a problem—It's a problem…because
I can't have a dog. Because, sometime in
your life, a dog got a little too happy
and, heaven forbid, knocked off a
Christmas ornament. That's what dogs

do: they get happy; they wag their tails.

MARIA
Exactly my point. Why are you back on this dog thing again?

JOE
Well, it's Christmas, Maria…

MARIA SHAKES HER HEAD AND ROLLS HER EYES.

MARIA
Joe? The lights?

JOE RISES AND PUTS ON HIS JACKET AS HE SPEAKS. HE LOOKS THROUGH THE DOORWAY INTO THE ROOM WHERE JOSH SLEEPS.

JOE
Maria? Josh is just a little guy right now…I mean, a dog is one thing but…You know—Christmas and everything, and next year he'll be, like, a toddler and…

MARIA
What are you saying?

JOE
I'm saying—I don't know what I'm saying.

I think I'm saying I don't know if Christmas is supposed to be as *tidy* as… Yeesh, I don't know what I'm saying. I'm saying every boy likes a dog. Don't forget that.

MARIA
Joe? The lights?

JOE EXITS, UPSTAGE RIGHT.

MARIA SHAKES HER HEAD AS JOE LEAVES.

MARIA
Why does this have to be difficult?

MARIA REACHES INTO A BOX AND PULLS OUT A BIG FAMILY BIBLE AND A BOOK STAND. SHE PLACES THE STAND ON THE TABLE NEXT TO JOE'S CHAIR.

MARIA OPENS THE BIBLE TO THE PAGE WHERE A RIBBON MARKS THE PLACE AND PUTS THE BIBLE ON THE STAND.

MARIA STEPS BACK TO LOOK AT THE ARRANGEMENT, SHAKES HER HEAD, PICKS UP THE BIBLE, SITS ON THE EDGE OF THE CHAIR AND BEGINS TO READ.

MARIA
Luke two, one. In those days Caesar Augustus issued a decree that a census should be taken of the entire Roman world. (This was the first census that took place while Quirinius was governor of Syria.) And everyone went to his own town to register.

So Joseph also went up from the town of Nazareth in Galilee to Judea, to Bethlehem the town of David, because he belonged to the house and line of David. He went there to register with Mary, who was *pledged to be married to him* and was *expecting a child*.

MARIA LOOKS OVER AT JOSH'S CRADLE. SHE CONTINUES.

While they were there, the time came for the baby to be born, and she gave birth to her firstborn, *a son*.

Maria rises and walks to the cradle as

she reads.

She wrapped him in cloths and *placed
him in a manger, because there was no room
for them in the inn.*

MARIA CLOSES THE BIBLE AND HUGS IT TO HER CHEST.

Dear God. That's awful.

MARIA BEGINS TO SING, SOFTLY, ACCOMPANIED BY GUITAR AND
FLUTE, *O COME O COME EMMANUEL.*

THE CONGREGATION IS DIRECTED TO JOIN THE SONG AS THE
ORGAN BEGINS ON THE SECOND VERSE.

MARY AND JOSEPH MAKE THEIR ENTRANCE FROM THE BACK AND
TAKE THEIR PLACE IN THE STABLE AS THE LIGHTS COME UP SOFTLY
AT STAGE LEFT.

THE SONG ENDS AND THE CONGREGATION IS QUIETED AS THE
ORGAN DROPS OUT AND THE FLUTE AND GUITAR CONTINUE
SOFTLY.

MARIA PUTS THE BIBLE ON THE TABLE AND PICKS UP BABY
JOSHUA. SHE MOVES TOWARD CENTER STAGE WITH HER CHILD.

MARY PICKS UP BABY JESUS AND MOVES TOWARD CENTER STAGE.

THE TWO SOFTLY REPRISE THE LAST PHRASE: "REJOICE, REJOICE,
EMMANUEL, HAS COME TO THEE, O ISRAEL."

FADE TO BLACK.

MARY RETURNS TO THE MANGER. MARIA SITS NEXT TO THE TREE.

THE CHOIR SINGS *CANDLES, CANDLES* AND *BLESSED IS HE WHO
COMES.*

HYMN: *LO, HOW A ROSE E'ER BLOOMING.*

FADE TO BLACK.

Scene Two

AS THE LIGHTS COME UP, MARIA IS IN A DAZE, ARRANGING A LARGISH MANGER SCENE NEAR THE CHRISTMAS TREE. SHE IS STARTLED WHEN JOE ENTERS WITH A PAPER BAG.

JOE
Hey, we've got a tree to decorate here!

MARIA
Hi. I, ah, was just, ah, working on the manger scene.

JOE TAKES OFF HIS JACKET.

JOE
Mmm. 'S cold out.

Ready to shed some more light on the subject?

MARIA
[absently]
Just about.

JOE
You ok? What's going on?

MARIA
I, ah…actually, I was reading the Bible and thinking…about Mary.

JOE
Mary Phillips? Give it up Maria—she'll never admit she was—

MARIA
[cutting in]
Not, Mary Phillips, Joe. Mary, the mother of Jesus.

JOE
Virgin Mary? Uh, Maria, it's December
fourth. Don't peak too soon, honey. You
won't have anything left for Christmas
Day.

MARIA
[flashing]
Joe…you're the reason some animals eat
their young!

MARIA EXITS HURRIEDLY. JOE SITS DOWN IN HIS CHAIR.

JOE
[mimicking under his breath]
You're the reason some animals eat their
young. Get a new line, Maria.

JOE LIFTS THE BIBLE FROM THE TABLE, STILL OPEN TO LUKE, CHAP-
TER TWO AND CONTINUES.

I told you not to read this without a
trained theologian present.

JOE LOOKS AT THE BEGINNING OF CHAPTER TWO, MUMBLING AS HE
SKIMS. HE BEGINS TO READ AND COMMENT AT VERSE EIGHT.

And there were shepherds living out in
the fields nearby, keeping watch over
their flocks at night. Shepherds—dirty
job, that.

An angel of the Lord appeared to them,
and the glory of the Lord shone around
them, and they were terrified.

I should say so. Nothing to fool around
with. [Yawn]

But the angel said to them, "Do not be
afraid. I bring you good news of great
joy that will be for all the people. Today
in the town of David a *Savior* has been
born to you; he is *Christ the Lord*."

The plot thickens…[big yawn]

"This will be a sign to you: You will find
a baby wrapped in cloths and lying in a
manger."

Lying in a manger. Imagine that…

JOE DRIFTS OFF TO SLEEP, STILL HOLDING THE BIBLE IN HIS HANDS.
THE LIGHTS DIM.

WE HEAR JOE READING LUKE 2:15-16 ON AUDIO CASSETTE AND
THE SHEPHERDS MAKE THEIR ENTRANCE AND COME TO THE
MANGER.

JOE (VOICE OVER)

When the angels had left them and gone
into heaven, the shepherds said to one
another, "Let's go to Bethlehem and see
this thing that has happened, which the
Lord has told us about."

So they hurried off and found Mary and
Joseph, and the baby, who was lying in
the manger.

THE CHOIR SINGS *HOSANNA IN THE HIGHEST*.

HYMN: *ANGELS WE HAVE HEARD ON HIGH*.

JOE'S SLEEP IS TROUBLED. HE GROANS AND SHUDDERS AND THE
BIBLE FALLS ONTO HIS CHEST. HE SETTLES AND WE HEAR LUKE
2:17-19 IN JOE'S VOICE.

JOE (VOICE OVER)
When they had seen him, they spread
the word concerning what had been told
them about this child, and all who heard
it were amazed at what the shepherds
said to them.

But Mary treasured up all these things
and pondered them in her heart.

THE CHOIR SINGS *HAIL THE TIDINGS*.

FADE TO BLACK.

Scene Three

AS THE LIGHTS COME UP, MARIA ARRIVES WITH A MUG OF COF-
FEE FOR JOE. HE UTTERS A LOUD GROAN AND SHE WAKES HIM. HE
IS STARTLED.

MARIA
Shh! You'll wake Joshua. What were you
dreaming?

JOE
Was I dreaming?

MARIA
I heard you all the way out in the
kitchen, angel.

JOE
You did not!

MARIA
I did! Something about shepherds washing their socks by night...

JOE

170

'S nothing. A mental note to pick up my
dry cleaning. Did you just call me *angel*?

MARIA

Why would I call you *angel*?

JOE

I *don't* know. I'm very confused about
that.

MARIA TAKES THE BIBLE OFF JOE'S CHEST AND BEGINS TURNING
BACK TO MATTHEW, CHAPTER TWO.

MARIA

Hmmm. Hey, can I read you something?

JOE

Not from there, no.

MARIA

No, seriously, Joe.

JOE

No, seriously, Maria.

MARIA HOLDS HIM IN HER GAZE AND HE SIGHS, THEN CONTINUES.

Ok. So read to me.

AS MARIA READS, THE MAGI MAKE THEIR ENTRANCE AND JOIN
THE SHEPHERDS AND MARY AND JOSEPH AT THE MANGER.

MARIA

Matthew, chapter two: After Jesus was
born in Bethlehem in Judea, during the
time of King Herod, Magi from the east
came to Jerusalem and asked, "Where is
the one who has been born king of the
Jews? We saw his star in the east and
have come to worship him."

Then Herod sent them to Bethlehem and said, "Go and make a careful search for the child. As soon as you find him, report to me."

After they had heard the king, they went on their way, and the star they had seen in the east went ahead of them until it stopped over the place where the child was.

When they saw the star, they were over-joyed.

MARIA HUGS THE BIBLE TO HER CHEST AND THE CHOIR SINGS *A STAR, A SONG*.

WHEN THE CHOIR IS FINISHED, MARIA CONTINUES.

That's what I want this year, Joe. I wanna be overjoyed that Jesus was born. I want us…I don't know. I just wanna do Christmas differently this year. *Better.* Look at this.

Joe takes the Bible from Maria and reads Matthew 2:11. As Joe reads, the Magi present their GIFTS to Jesus.

JOE
On coming to the house, they saw the child with his mother Mary, and they bowed down and worshiped him. Then they opened their treasures and present-ed him with gifts of gold and of incense and of myrrh.

MARIA
Could we do that, Joe? Could we give a gift to Jesus this Christmas?

                    JOE
        Like, a birthday present?

                   MARIA
        Yeh, like a birthday present.

LIGHTS DIM.

THE CHOIR SINGS *NOEL, THE OX AND THE DONKEY'S CAROL.*

LIGHTS UP FULL.

                    JOE
        Maria…Can I tell you the truth about
        me and Christmas?

                   MARIA
        You bet.

                    JOE
        Christmas has never seemed very *real* to
        me. It's more a *family* thing, you know?
        And I haven't always done so well with
        family things.

                   MARIA
        I know.

                    JOE
        But I want to.

                   MARIA
        I know that too.

        And I get so caught up in the details —

JOE
[cutting in]
No, baby, it's okay. We don't have to
turn this into a guilt-fest. I'm still guilty
about not being thankful on
Thanksgiving.

MARIA
That's funny. You ate turkey like you
were thankful.

JOE
I ate turkey like I was starving.

Which is why I like the idea of a birthday present for Jesus. On Thanksgiving,
I eat like a man who doesn't have
enough food —

MARIA
[cutting in]
And I do Christmas gifts like a woman
who doesn't have enough stuff.

JOE
But I do have enough stuff.

MARIA
Yeh. Me too…

JOE
[shrugging]
Brave words on December fourth.

MARIA
No, I'm not saying we should go cold
turkey —

JOE
[cutting in]
Please: enough turkey.

MARIA
[finishing]
I'm just saying, can we think about a
gift for Jesus? Something he would
appreciate…

JOE LOOKS AROUND AS IF HE WAS LOOKING FOR SOMEONE TO
OBJECT.

JOE
We're in charge, Maria. We can do
whatever's right. Hey, do you suppose
Jesus might like a puppy? I'd be glad to
keep it at my house.

LIGHTS DIM.

THE CHOIR SINGS *THE GIFT*.

LIGHTS BACK UP.

JOE READS THE BIBLE SILENTLY AND MARIA GOES TO LOOK AT HER
CHILD.

MARIA PICKS UP JOSHUA AND MOVES TOWARDS CENTER STAGE
WHERE SHE BEGINS TO SING *MANGER CAROL* WITH SIMPLE ACCOM-
PANIMENT.

THE CHOIR JOINS HER ON THE REFRAIN.

MARY MOVES CENTER STAGE WITH HER BABY AND SINGS THE SEC-
OND VERSE. THE CHOIR JOINS THE REFRAIN.

MARIA AND MARY ALTERNATE VERSES AND JUST THE TWO OF
THEM REPEAT THE REFRAIN AT THE END.

FADE TO BLACK.

LIGHTS COME UP FOR *SILENT NIGHT* AND CANDLE-LIGHTING.

AT THE END OF THE CANDLE-LIGHTING, MARIA GESTURES TO JOE THAT HE SHOULD COVER HIS EYES. SHE GOES TO THE WINGS AND RETURNS WITH A LARGE BOX. JOE OPENS THE BOX ON THE FLOOR AND HIS FACE REGISTERS SURPRISE AND HAPPINESS. HE PULLS OUT A PUPPY AND, AFTER A BEAT, PULLS OUT A SECOND PUPPY.

FADE TO BLACK.